WILLIAM JENNINGS BRYAN
AND THE CAMPAIGN OF 1896

Problems in American Civilization

UNDER THE EDITORIAL DIRECTION OF *George Rogers Taylor*

PURITANISM IN EARLY AMERICA

THE CAUSES OF THE AMERICAN REVOLUTION, *Revised*

BENJAMIN FRANKLIN AND THE AMERICAN CHARACTER

THE DECLARATION OF INDEPENDENCE AND THE CONSTITUTION, *Revised*

HAMILTON AND THE NATIONAL DEBT

THE TURNER THESIS CONCERNING THE ROLE OF THE FRONTIER IN
    AMERICAN HISTORY, *Revised*

THE WAR OF 1812—PAST JUSTIFICATIONS AND PRESENT INTERPRETATIONS

THE GREAT TARIFF DEBATE, 1820–1830

THE MEANING OF JACKSONIAN DEMOCRACY

THE REMOVAL OF THE CHEROKEE NATION—MANIFEST DESTINY OR
    NATIONAL DISHONOR?

JACKSON VERSUS BIDDLE—THE STRUGGLE OVER THE SECOND BANK OF THE
    UNITED STATES

THE TRANSCENDENTALIST REVOLT AGAINST MATERIALISM

THE COMPROMISE OF 1850

THE CAUSES OF THE AMERICAN CIVIL WAR

SLAVERY AS A CAUSE OF THE CIVIL WAR, *Revised*

LINCOLN AND THE COMING OF THE CIVIL WAR

THE AMERICANNESS OF WALT WHITMAN

RECONSTRUCTION IN THE SOUTH

MARK TWAIN'S *Huckleberry Finn*

DEMOCRACY AND THE GOSPEL OF WEALTH

JOHN D. ROCKEFELLER—ROBBER BARON OR INDUSTRIAL STATESMAN?

THE PULLMAN BOYCOTT OF 1894—THE PROBLEM OF FEDERAL
    INTERVENTION

BOOKER T. WASHINGTON AND HIS CRITICS—THE PROBLEM OF NEGRO
    LEADERSHIP

WILLIAM JENNINGS BRYAN AND THE CAMPAIGN OF 1896

AMERICAN IMPERIALISM IN 1898

ROOSEVELT, WILSON, AND THE TRUSTS

PRAGMATISM AND AMERICAN CULTURE

WILSON AT VERSAILLES

THE NEW DEAL—REVOLUTION OR EVOLUTION? *Revised*

FRANKLIN D. ROOSEVELT AND THE SUPREME COURT

PEARL HARBOR—ROOSEVELT AND THE COMING OF THE WAR

THE YALTA CONFERENCE

INDUSTRY-WIDE COLLECTIVE BARGAINING—PROMISE OR MENACE?

EDUCATION FOR DEMOCRACY—THE DEBATE OVER THE REPORT OF THE
    PRESIDENT'S COMMISSION ON HIGHER EDUCATION

EVOLUTION AND RELIGION—THE CONFLICT BETWEEN SCIENCE AND
    THEOLOGY IN MODERN AMERICA

IMMIGRATION—AN AMERICAN DILEMMA

LOYALTY IN A DEMOCRATIC STATE

DESEGREGATION AND THE SUPREME COURT

WILLIAM JENNINGS BRYAN
AND THE CAMPAIGN OF 1896

EDITED WITH AN INTRODUCTION BY

George F. Whicher

Problems in American Civilization

READINGS SELECTED BY THE
DEPARTMENT OF AMERICAN STUDIES
AMHERST COLLEGE

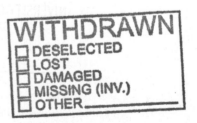
D. C. HEATH AND COMPANY: Boston

INTRODUCTION

"Bryan or McKinley — which are you for?"

The six-year-old boy had no idea. He had never heard either name before. But around him stood his gang, the boys who lived on a certain block in Brooklyn, suddenly menacing. Evidently it was required of him to choose. He faltered, "Bryan." Instantly every throat was opened against him. He was jostled, kicked, punched, until he recanted in tears. Then and there he was enlisted in the Republican ranks and pledged to support the gold standard. Soon he was happily yelling with the others:

> McKinley drinks so-da-wa-ter,
> Bryan drinks *rum*;
> McKinley is a gen-tle-man,
> Bryan is a BUM!

At the same time in Springfield, Illinois, a youngster named Nicholas Vachel Lindsay, aged sixteen, found himself and his gang committed heart and soul to Free Silver and the "Boy Orator of the Platte,"

> Defying aristocracy,
> With every bridle gone,
> Ridding the world of the low down mean,
> Bidding the eagles of the West fly on.

To him Bryan was a new messiah, champion of the plain people, bard and prophet of democracy, prairie avenger, gigantic troubadour, speaking like a siege gun.

In 1896 traditional party lines were giving way. There were Silver Republicans in Colorado, Gold Democrats in New York. Farmers of the West and South were lined up against the money-lending East. Not for a long time had political passions been so deeply stirred. Vachel Lindsay rightly held that "there were real heads broken in the fustian and the rattle." The ostensible conflict over silver and gold screened the clash of mighty opposites.

To economists a nation's monetary system, including the question of bimetallism, still remains a debatable issue, but hardly one to break heads over. In 1792 Congress provided for the minting of gold and silver coins at the ratio of 15 to 1 and both coins were made legal tender. This ratio was changed to 16 to 1 during the 1830's, and in 1873, when the coinage laws were being revised, no provision was made for continuing the silver dollar as a legal tender coin. Then, for technical reasons connected with foreign exchange, Congress declared the gold dollar the single unit of value. No immediate disaster ensued, but some fifteen years later when prices of farm products were abysmally low the agricultural interests fixed upon the failure to include the silver dollar as a full legal tender coin as the prime reason why money had become so scarce. The so-called demonetization of silver then became known as "the crime of 1873." The Democrats took up the slogan of Free Silver as a panacea for every social ill, while the Republicans rejected it as equivalent to repudiation of debts and a long step on the road to ruin.

It was not the controversy over the currency, however, which led Professor Harry Thurston Peck, a seasoned man about town in New York, to call the campaign of 1896 "the most eventful political struggle which the people of the United States had witnessed since that which ended in the first election of Abraham Lincoln." Consciously or not, the voters were deciding what kind of country they wanted their America to be.

Much the same grass-roots democracy that had given support to Jefferson and Jackson and Lincoln rallied at the call of Bryan. He was, says Professor Commager, "the last great spokesman of the America of the nineteenth century — of the America of the Middle West and the South, the America of the farm and the country town, the America that read its Bible and went to Chautauqua, distrusted the big city and Wall Street, believed in God and the Declaration of Independence." Bryan was completely identified with the frontier agrarianism which frequently at times of crisis had exercised a decisive control over the nation's policies. The campaign of 1896 seemed like a renewal of a perennial conflict, as old as Shays' Rebellion, between producers and exploiters, debtors and creditors. To hard-pressed farmers Bryan's program of financial relief roused hopes of a new birth of freedom.

But during the long period of Republican domination from Grant to Harrison new forces had quietly risen to power. Great industries developed in steel, oil, copper, coal, and huge corporations came into being to promote them. The rapid expansion of railroads produced a revolution in transportation. More and more people were crowding to the cities. Many men whose fathers had been independent small farmers, tradesmen, or artisans found employment in factories and swelled the ranks of wage-earners. The control of the country's economy tended to pass out of the hands of producers and operators and to be assumed by a managerial elite responsible to financiers and stockholders. Urbanism, the complex of attitudes fostered by a highly industrialized, competitive society, was accepted as standard. The prophet of industrial competition and the concentration of wealth was Herbert Spencer, whose creed of social Darwinism taught a literal application to human affairs of the evolutionary concept of "the survival of the fittest." Through the Republican party, captains of industry had ruled the country for twenty-five years, favoring the manufacturing interests by means of protective tariffs. Mark Hanna, an Ohio businessman in politics, intended to see to it that they did not lose their grip.

In "Under the Lion's Paw" Hamlin Garland significantly portrays the two ideologies side by side. When the Haskins family, defeated by grasshoppers in Kansas, arrived in Rock River looking for a place to settle, they are befriended in neighborly western fashion by Stephen Council and his wife. The newcomers are boarded and lodged for a season, located on a farm that can be restocked and reconditioned, and encouraged to make a new start in life, all without any thought of payment for the service. The frontier agrarian tradition implied a willingness to help each other on the part of men engaged in a common struggle with the forces of nature. But the old tradition is now on the wane and a fiercely acquisitive spirit, which frontier conditions had done nothing to discourage, is coming to the fore, reinforced by ideas of laissez faire. Jim Butler, the landholder who takes sharp advantage of Haskins' trustfulness, is not merely a skinflint by nature.

He is the representative of a society conducted on strictly business principles, where there is no room for careless generosity and where every man is presumed to be armed against his neighbor.

The contrast, as Garland presents it, is weighted against the new commercialism. Not all men who flourished in business were mean-spirited gougers of the Butler type. Henry James draws a very different portrait of a California businessman in *The American*. But the code of ethics enforced in business circles was notably more lax than the personal morality characteristic of the farm and the small town. The difference is perceptively illustrated by William Dean Howells at the turning point of his novel, *The Rise of Silas Lapham*, where the New England conscience of Silas will not allow him to make an overreaching business deal which would have saved his fortune.

Between the Civil War and the end of the century the welfare of the growers of staple crops such as wheat, corn, and cotton was seriously neglected. The opening up of rich Western lands led to the harvesting of a few bonanza crops. Land speculation inevitably followed. A cycle of drought years, grasshopper plagues, and falling prices made farming for a profit impossible in many sections of the country. Though a Department of Agriculture was created by Congress in 1862, its head did not become a cabinet officer until 1889. There was no organized farm bloc, no system of government loans, and the idea of federal support of farm prices was not yet dreamed of. The farmer had no recourse but to borrow money on ruinous terms. More capital was needed than could be found locally, and for a time farm mortgages at ten per cent or better were highly attractive to Eastern investors. When the farmer found it impossible to pay off his mortgage, the East be-

gan to look very much like Uncle Shylock. The heavily indebted sections of the country were not concerned to support the value of the dollar for the convenience of bankers; they wanted a fair price for their wheat and cotton.

The plight of the Western farmers was discussed from two different standpoints by Washington Gladden in 1890 and by James Laurence Laughlin in 1896. The former, a Congregational minister and free-lance journalist widely interested in social problems, took a sympathetic interest in the economic difficulties under which the farmers were suffering and listed a number of radical proposals for remedial action without condemning any of them as socialistic. Professor Laughlin, the recently appointed head of the department of political economy at the University of Chicago, was a classically trained historian and economist who had already published a *History of Bimetallism in the United States* (1886). As the champion of a fixed gold standard, regardless of the fact that the value of gold itself is subject to fluctuation, Laughlin viewed the causes of agricultural discontent from a somewhat theoretical standpoint. His bland assumption that Western farming must go out of business if it was unable to meet competition in the world market was not calculated to soothe farmers who were not too "undereducated" to know that American manufacturers were being protected against foreign competition by carefully rigged tariffs.

Various measures, some of them political, had been proposed to deliver the farmer from the mounting burden of debt. Early in the 1870's the Greenback party agitated for the continued issue of unsupported paper money with the idea that a depreciating currency would make it easier for debtors to meet their obligations. At about the same time or even earlier the Granger movement organized cooperative agencies for the storage and sale of farm products. The Grangers also worked for reforms, such as the regulation of railroad rates, to protect the farmer from profiteers. With the formation of the Farmer's Alliances or People's party, later known as the Populists, in the latter 1800's, the agrarian movement became a serious factor in national politics. Making common cause with labor and with socialist elements among the foreign born, the Populists threatened to rise to power as the Republicans had risen on the eve of the Civil War. In the election of 1890 they were able to carry a dozen Western and Southern states and to seat twenty or more Senators and Representatives in Congress. Two years later the Populist candidate for President polled over a million votes. It seemed possible that the Populists might replace the moribund Democrats as the second major party, a party pledged to reform and a fair deal for the working man of the nation.

A few sentences from the preamble of the Populist Platform, written by a devoted agrarian reformer named Ignatius Donnelly and adopted with acclaim at St. Louis in February, 1892, will suggest the highly overcharged atmosphere of the time:

We meet in the midst of a nation brought to the verge of moral, political and material ruin. . . . The fruits of the toil of millions are boldly stolen to build up colossal fortunes, unprecedented in the history of the world, while their possessors despise the republic and endanger liberty. . . . The national power to create money is appropriated to enrich bondholders; silver, which has been accepted as coin since the dawn of history, has been demonetized to add to the purchasing power of gold by decreasing the value of all forms of property as well as human labor; and the

supply of currency is purposely abridged to fatten usurers, bankrupt enterprise and enslave industry. A vast conspiracy against mankind has been organized on two continents and is taking possession of the world. . . .

The Populists proceeded to demand, among other reforms, the free and unlimited coinage of silver, a graduated income tax, postal savings banks, and government ownership of railroads, telegraph, and telephone.

Between 1892 and 1896, while the farmers grew ever more desperate, there was further deterioration in the general situation. The savage treatment of the striking steel workers at the Homestead mills, the uncalled-for intervention of federal troops in the Pullman strike and the imprisonment of the labor leader Eugene V. Debs, made the working classes ripe for revolt. The panic of 1893 was followed by a period of unemployment. Coxey's "army" and other groups of men out of work marched on Washington. The old-line parties did nothing to remove the causes of unrest. The Democrats were paralyzed by internal dissensions. Meanwhile the Republicans under the guidance of Mark Hanna nominated a respectable Ohio politician for the presidency and prepared for a routine campaign on the tariff issue. The Populist leaders felt that their great opportunity was at hand.

The story of how the Democrats unexpectedly repudiated the leadership of President Cleveland, took over the Free Silver issue from the Populists, and nominated the young Nebraska spellbinder, William Jennings Bryan, is well told in the chapter quoted from Matthew Josephson. There may be found also the salient passages from Bryan's famous "Cross of Gold" speech at the Chicago convention, and an account of the progress of the campaign week by week until the morning after the election. An editorial from the *Nation,* presumably written by the enlightened E. L. Godkin, indicates the violence with which the conservative East reacted to the news of Bryan's nomination. A chapter from Herbert Croly's *Marcus Alonzo Hanna* gives a detailed analysis of the extreme measures taken by the Republicans to make McKinley's election doubly sure. And from the historical perspective of more than half a century James A. Barnes re-examines the forces in conflict and appraises anew the significance of the struggle.

There follow four selections which undertake to assess the quality of Bryan's leadership. Charles E. Merriam, a professor of history, and H. L. Mencken, the well-known editor and critic, writing immediately after Bryan's death, give almost diametrically opposite estimates of his worth. Approximately twenty years later Professor Commager composes a brief appreciation of Bryan as an American political leader, while Richard Hofstadter systematically reviews all the evidence in an effort to reach a lasting historical verdict on the Great Commoner.

No account of Bryan's importance at the turn of the century can afford to ignore the tremendous upsurge of emotion that the campaign of 1896 aroused. To get some idea of this we must turn to Vachel Lindsay's "Bryan, Bryan, Bryan, Bryan," which vividly recalls the very forms and pressures of the moment. The poem preserves for posterity, as if in amber, the attitudes and intensities of feeling that marked the agrarian crusade against the power of gold.

Many highly intelligent citizens and men of good will felt as they read the election returns on November 4, 1896, that the country had narrowly escaped from disaster. For four months nearly every newspaper in the land had been denouncing Bryan as an anarchist and a menace to the stability of the republic. Hanna's success in placing McKinley in the White House prolonged for five years the era of "stand pat" Republicanism. A return of prosperity and an increase in the world's supply of gold did something to ease the hard times and to put off for a little the inevitable day of reckoning. Then the war with Spain distracted attention from domestic problems. But with the assassination of McKinley in 1901 the system of things for which he stood came to an end. His successor, it was often remarked, not infrequently took a leaf from Bryan's book without bothering to give credit.

As we look back across the administrations of Truman and Franklin Roosevelt, Woodrow Wilson, and Theodore Roosevelt, the measures of reform proposed by the Bryanites do not seem very alarming. Most of them, in fact, have been enacted into law. Though Bryan lost what he called "the First Battle," the cause he supported was to triumph under other leaders. Are we to think of him, then, as a prophet who prepared the way for the liberal progressive movement of the twentieth century, the first American statesman to foresee the Welfare State as it is being developed today? Or was he simply a shallow demagogue whose sudden rise to prominence in 1896 confused the real issues and prevented the sound growth of a reform party which could rally both urban laborers and dispossessed farmers? [NOTE: The Bryan quote in the Clash of Issues on page xii was quoted in Paxton Hibben, *The Peerless Leader, William Jennings Bryan* (New York: Farrar & Rinehart, Inc., 1929), p. 168.]

CONTENTS

		PAGE
1	HAMLIN GARLAND *Under the Lion's Paw*	1
2	WASHINGTON GLADDEN *The Embattled Farmers*	9
3	JAMES LAURENCE LAUGHLIN *Causes of Agricultural Unrest*	15
4	EDITORIAL *The Chicago Nominee*	24
5	MATTHEW JOSEPHSON *The Bryan Campaign*	26
6	HERBERT CROLY *The Campaign of 1896*	56
7	JAMES A. BARNES *Myths of the Bryan Campaign*	68
8	CHARLES E. MERRIAM *William Jennings Bryan*	78
9	HENRY LOUIS MENCKEN *In Memoriam: W. J. B.*	82
10	HENRY STEELE COMMAGER *William Jennings Bryan*	87
11	RICHARD HOFSTADTER *The Democrat as Revivalist*	89
12	VACHEL LINDSAY *Bryan, Bryan, Bryan, Bryan*	102
	Suggestions for Additional Reading	107

THE CLASH OF ISSUES

If the gold standard advocates win, this country will be dominated by the financial harpies of Wall Street. I am trying to save the American people from that disaster — which will mean the enslavement of the farmers, merchants, manufacturers and laboring classes to the most merciless and unscrupulous gang of speculators on earth — the money power. My ambition is to make money the *servant* of industry, to dethrone it from the false position it has usurped as *master,* and this can only be done by destroying the money monopoly.

— WILLIAM JENNINGS BRYAN

He goes down with the cause and must abide with it in the history of infamy. He had less provocation than Benedict Arnold, less intellectual force than Aaron Burr, less manliness and courage than Jefferson Davis. He was the rival of them all in deliberate wickedness and treason to the Republic. — NEW YORK TRIBUNE, *November 4, 1896*

Election night at midnight:
Boy Bryan's defeat.
Defeat of western silver.
Defeat of the wheat.

. . . . .

Defeat of tornadoes by the poison vats supreme.
Defeat of my boyhood, defeat of my dream.

— VACHEL LINDSAY

For Bryan was the last great spokesman of the America of the nineteenth century — of the America of the Middle West and the South, the America of the farm and the country town, the America that read its Bible and went to Chautauqua, distrusted the big city and Wall Street, believed in God and the Declaration of Independence.

— HENRY STEELE COMMAGER

The chances are that history will put the peak of democracy in America in his time; it has been on the downward curve among us since the campaign of 1896. He will be remembered perhaps, as its supreme impostor, the *reductio ad absurdum* of its pretension.

— HENRY LOUIS MENCKEN

He could no more analyze the issues of his day than the Confederates could realize the obsolescence of slavery.

— RICHARD HOFSTADTER

What his enemies could not understand was that the people are as much interested in knowing about their leader's heart as in knowing about his head, and that sympathy no less than intelligence plays its part in the great process of popular control.

— CHARLES E. MERRIAM

Hamlin Garland: UNDER THE LION'S PAW

IT was the last of autumn and first day of winter coming together. All day long the ploughmen on their prairie farms had moved to and fro in their wide level fields through the falling snow, which melted as it fell, wetting them to the skin — all day, notwithstanding the frequent squalls of snow, the dripping, desolate clouds, and the muck of the furrows, black and tenacious as tar.

Under their dripping harness the horses swung to and fro silently, with that marvellous uncomplaining patience which marks the horse. All day the wild geese, honking wildly, as they sprawled sidewise down the wind, seemed to be fleeing from an enemy behind, and with neck outthrust and wings extended, sailed down the wind, soon lost to sight.

Yet the ploughman behind his plough, though the snow lay on his ragged greatcoat, and the cold clinging mud rose on his heavy boots, fettering him like gyves, whistled in the very beard of the gale. As day passed, the snow, ceasing to melt, lay along the ploughed land, and lodged in the depth of the stubble, till on each slow round the last furrow stood out black and shining as jet between the ploughed land and the gray stubble.

When night began to fall, and the geese, flying low, began to alight invisibly in the near corn-field, Stephen Council was still at work "finishing a land." He rode on his sulky plough when going with the wind, but walked when facing it. Sitting bent and cold but cheery under his slouch hat, he talked encouragingly to his four-in-hand.

"Come round there, boys! — Round again! We got t' finish this land. Come in there, Dan! *Stiddy,* Kate, — stiddy! None o' y'r tantrums, Kittie. It's purty tuff, but got a be did. *Tchk! tchk!* Step along, Pete! Don't let Kate git y'r singletree on the wheel. Once more!"

They seemed to know what he meant, and that this was the last round, for they worked with greater vigor than before.

"Once more, boys, an' then, sez I, oats an' a nice warm stall, an' sleep f'r all."

By the time the last furrow was turned on the land it was too dark to see the house, and the snow was changing to rain again. The tired and hungry man could see the light from the kitchen shining through the leafless hedge, and he lifted a great shout, "Supper f'r a half a dozen!"

It was nearly eight o'clock by the time he had finished his chores and started for supper. He was picking his way carefully through the mud, when the tall form of a man loomed up before him with a premonitory cough.

"Waddy ye want?" was the rather startled question of the farmer.

"Well, ye see," began the stranger, in a deprecating tone, "we'd like t' git f'r the night. We've tried every house f'r the last two miles, but they hadn't any room f'r us. My wife's jest about sick, 'n' the children are cold and hungry — "

"Oh, y' want 'o stay all night, eh?"

"Yes, sir; it 'ud be a great accom — "

"Wall, I don't make it a practice t' turn anybuddy way hungry, not on sech nights as this. Drive right in. We ain't got much, but sech as it is — "

Hamlin Garland, *Main-Travelled Roads* (New York: Harper and Brothers, 1891), pp. 197–217.

But the stranger had disappeared. And soon his steaming, weary team, with drooping heads and swinging single-trees, moved past the well to the block beside the path. Council stood at the side of the "schooner" and helped the children out — two little half-sleeping children — and then a small woman with a babe in her arms.

"There ye go!" he shouted jovially, to the children. "Now we're all right! Run right along to the house there, an' tell Mam' Council you wants sumpthin' t' eat. Right this way, Mis' — keep right off t' the right there. I'll go an' git a lantern. Come," he said to the dazed and silent group at his side.

"Mother," he shouted, as he neared the fragrant and warmly lighted kitchen, "here are some wayfarers an' folks who need sumpthin' t' eat an' a place t' snooze." He ended by pushing them all in.

Mrs. Council, a large, jolly, rather coarse-looking woman, took the children in her arms. "Come right in, you little rabbits. 'Most asleep, hey? Now here's a drink o' milk f'r each o' ye. I'll have s'm tea in a minute. Take off y'r things and set up t' the fire."

While she set the children to drinking milk, Council got out his lantern and went out to the barn to help the stranger about his team, where his loud, hearty voice could be heard as it came and went between the haymow and the stalls.

The woman came to light as a small, timid, and discouraged-looking woman, but still pretty, in a thin and sorrowful way.

"Land sakes! An' you've travelled all the way from Clear Lake t'-day in this mud! Waal! waal! No wonder you're all tired out. Don't wait f'r the men, 'Mis' — " She hesitated, waiting for the name.

"Haskins."

"Mis' Haskins, set right up to the table an' take a good swig o' tea whilst I make y' s'm toast. It's green tea, an' it's good. I tell Council as I git older I don't seem to enjoy Young Hyson n'r Gunpowder. I want the reel green tea, jest as it comes off'n the vines. Seems t' have more heart in it, some way. Don't s'pose it has. Council says it's all in m' eye."

Going on in this easy way, she soon had the children filled with bread and milk and the woman thoroughly at home, eating some toast and sweet-melon pickles, and sipping the tea.

"See the little rats!" she laughed at the children. "They're full as they can stick now, and they want to go to bed. Now, don't get up, Mis' Haskins; set right where you are an' let me look after 'em. I know all about young ones, though I'm all alone now. Jane went an' married last fall. But, as I tell Council, it's lucky we keep our health. Set right there, Mis' Haskins; I won't have you stir a finger."

It was an unmeasured pleasure to sit there in the warm, homely kitchen, the jovial chatter of the housewife driving out and holding at bay the growl of the impotent, cheated wind.

The little woman's eyes filled with tears which fell down upon the sleeping baby in her arms. The world was not so desolate and cold and hopeless, after all.

"Now I hope Council won't stop out there and talk politics all night. He's the greatest man to talk politics an' read the Tribune — How old is it?"

She broke off and peered down at the face of the babe.

"Two months 'n' five days," said the mother, with a mother's exactness.

"Ye don't say! I want 'o know! The dear little pudzy-wudzy!" she went on, stirring it up in the neighborhood of the ribs with her fat forefinger.

"Pooty tough on 'oo to go gallivant'n' 'cross lots this way — "

"Yes, that's so; a man can't lift a mountain," said Council, entering the door. "Mother, this is Mr. Haskins, from Kansas. He's been eat up 'n' drove out by grasshoppers."

"Glad t' see yeh! — Pa, empty that wash-basin 'n' give him a chance t' wash."

Haskins was a tall man, with a thin, gloomy face. His hair was a reddish brown, like his coat, and seemed equally faded by the wind and sun, and his sallow face, though hard and set, was pathetic somehow. You would have felt that he had suffered much by the line of his mouth showing under his thin, yellow mustache.

"Hain't Ike got home yet, Sairy?"

"Hain't seen 'im."

"W-a-a-l, set right up, Mr. Haskins; wade right into what we've got; 'tain't much, but we manage to live on it — she gits fat on it," laughed Council, pointing his thumb at his wife.

After supper, while the women put the children to bed, Haskins and Council talked on, seated near the huge cooking-stove, the steam rising from their wet clothing. In the Western fashion Council told as much of his own life as he drew from his guest. He asked but few questions, but by and by the story of Haskins' struggles and defeat came out. The story was a terrible one, but he told it quietly, seated with his elbows on his knees, gazing most of the time at the hearth.

"I didn't like the looks of the country, anyhow," Haskins said, partly rising and glancing at his wife. "I was ust t' northern Ingyannie, where we have lots o' timber 'n' lots o' rain, 'n' I didn't like the looks o' that dry prairie. What galled me the worst was goin' s' far away acrosst so much fine land laying all through here vacant."

"And the 'hoppers eat ye four years, hand runnin', did they?"

"Eat! They wiped us out. They chawed everything that was green. They jest set around waitin' f'r us to die t' eat us, too. My God! I ust t' dream of 'em sittin' 'round on the bedpost, six feet long, workin' their jaws. They eet the fork-handles. They got worse 'n' worse till they jest rolled on one another, piled up like snow in winter. Well, it ain't no use. If I was t' talk all winter I couldn't tell nawthin'. But all the while I couldn't help thinkin' of all that land back here that nobuddy was usin' that I ought 'o had 'stead o' bein' out there in that cussed country."

"Waal, why didn't ye stop an' settle here?" asked Ike, who had come in and was eating his supper.

"Fer the simple reason that you fellers wantid ten 'r fifteen dollars an acre fer the bare land, and I hadn't no money fer that kind o' thing."

"Yes, I do my own work," Mrs. Council was heard to say in the pause which followed. "I'm a gettin' purty heavy t' be on m' laigs all day, but we can't afford t' hire, so I keep rackin' around somehow, like a foundered horse. S' lame — I tell Council he can't tell how lame I am, f'r I'm jest as lame in one laig as t'other." And the good soul laughed at the joke on herself as she took a handful of flour and dusted the biscuit-board to keep the dough from sticking.

"Well, I hain't never been very strong," said Mrs. Haskins. "Our folks was Canadians an' small-boned, and then since my last child I hain't got up again fairly. I don't like t' complain. Tim has about all he can bear now — but they was days this week when I jest wanted to lay right down an' die."

"Waal, now, I'll tell ye," said Council, from his side of the stove, silencing everybody with his good-natured roar, "I'd go down and see Butler, anyway, if I was you. I guess he'd let you have his place purty cheap; the farm's all run down. He's ben anxious t' let t' somebuddy next year. It 'ud be a good chance fer you. Anyhow, you go to bed and sleep like a babe. I've got some ploughin' t' do, anyhow, an' we'll see if somethin' can't be done about your case. Ike, you go out an' see if the horses is all right, an' I'll show the folks t' bed."

When the tired husband and wife were lying under the generous quilts of the spare bed, Haskins listened a moment to the wind in the eaves, and then said, with a slow and solemn tone,

"There are people in this world who are good enough t' be angels, an' only haff t' die to be angels."

II

Jim Butler was one of those men called in the West "land poor." Early in the history of Rock River he had come into the town and started in the grocery business in a small way, occupying a small building in a mean part of the town. At this period of his life he earned all he got, and was up early and late sorting beans, working over butter, and carting his goods to and from the station. But a change came over him at the end of the second year, when he sold a lot of land for four times what he paid for it. From that time forward he believed in land speculation as the surest way of getting rich. Every cent he could save or spare from his trade he put into land at forced sale, or mortgages on land, which were "just as good as the wheat," he was accustomed to say.

Farm after farm fell into his hands, until he was recognized as one of the leading landowners of the county. His mortgages were scattered all over Cedar County, and as they slowly but surely fell in he sought usually to retain the former owner as tenant.

He was not ready to foreclose; indeed, he had the name of being one of the "easiest" men in the town. He let the debtor off again and again, extending the time whenever possible.

"I don't want y'r land," he said. "All I'm after is the int'rest on my money — that's all. Now, if y' want 'o stay on the farm, why, I'll give y' a good chance. I can't have the land layin' vacant." And in many cases the owner remained as tenant.

In the meantime he had sold his store; he couldn't spend time in it; he was mainly occupied now with sitting around town on rainy days smoking and "gassin' with the boys," or in riding to and from his farms. In fishing-time he fished a good deal. Doc Grimes, Ben Ashley, and Cal Cheatham were his cronies on these fishing excursions or hunting trips in the time of chickens or partridges. In winter they went to Northern Wisconsin to shoot deer.

In spite of all these signs of easy life Butler persisted in saying he "hadn't enough money to pay taxes on his land," and was careful to convey the impression that he was poor in spite of his twenty farms. At one time he was said to be worth fifty thousand dollars, but land had been a little slow of sale of late, so that he was not worth so much.

A fine farm, known as the Higley place, had fallen into his hands in the usual way the previous year, and he had not been able to find a tenant for it. Poor Higley, after working himself nearly to death on it in the attempt to lift the mortgage, had gone off to Dakota, leaving the farm and his curse to Butler.

This was the farm which Council advised Haskins to apply for: and the next day Council hitched up his team and drove down town to see Butler.

"You jest let *me* do the talkin'," he said. "We'll find him wearin' out his pants on some salt barrel somew'ers; and if he thought you *wanted* a place he'd sock it to you hot and heavy. You jest keep quiet; I'll fix 'im."

Butler was seated in Ben Ashley's store telling fish yarns when Council sauntered in casually.

"Hello, But; lyin' agin, hey?"

"Hello, Steve! how goes it?"

"Oh, so-so. Too dang much rain these days. I thought it was goin' t' freeze up f'r good last night. Tight squeak if I get m' ploughin' done. How's farmin' with you these days?"

"Bad. Ploughin' ain't half done."

"It 'ud be a religious idee f'r you t' go out an' take a hand y'rself."

"I don't haff to," said Butler, with a wink.

"Got anybody on the Higley place?"

"No. Know of anybody?"

"Waal, no; not eggsackly. I've got a relation back t' Michigan who's ben hot an' cold on the idee o' comin' West f'r some time. Might come if he could get a good lay-out. What do you talk on the farm?"

"Well, I d' know. I'll rent it on shares or I'll rent it money rent."

"Waal, how much money, say?"

"Well, say ten per cent, on the price — two fifty."

"Waal, that ain't bad. Wait on 'im till 'e thrashes?"

Haskins listened eagerly to his important question, but Council was coolly eating a dried apple which he had speared out of a barrel with his knife. Butler studied him carefully.

"Well, knocks me out of twenty-five dollars interest."

"My relation'll need all he's got t' git his crops in," said Council, in the safe, indifferent way.

"Well, all right; say wait," concluded Butler.

"All right; this is the man. Haskins, this is Mr. Butler — no relation to Ben — the hardest-working man in Cedar County."

On the way home Haskins said: "I ain't much better off. I'd like that farm; it's a good farm, but it's all run down, an' so 'm I. I could make a good farm of it if I had half a show. But I can't stock it n'r seed it."

"Waal, now, don't you worry," roared Council in his ear. "We'll pull y' through somehow till next harvest. He's agreed t' hire it ploughed, an' you can earn a hundred dollars ploughin' an' y' c'n get the seed o' me, an' pay me back when y' can."

Haskins was silent with emotion, but at last he said, "I ain't got nothin' t' live on."

"Now, don't you worry 'bout that. You jest make your headquarters at ol' Steve Council's. Mother'll take a pile o' comfort in havin' y'r wife an' children 'round. Y' see, Jane's married off lately, an' Ike's away a good 'eal, so we'll be darn glad t' have y' stop with us this winter. Nex' spring we'll see if y' can't get a start again." And he chirruped to the team, which sprang forward with the rumbling, clattering wagon.

"Say, looky here, Council, you can't do this. I never saw — " shouted Haskins in his neighbor's ear.

Council moved about uneasily in his seat and stopped his stammering gratitude by saying: "Hold on, now; don't make such a fuss over a little thing. When I see a man down, an' things all on top of 'im, I jest like t' kick em off an' help 'm up. That's the kind of religion I got, an' it's about the only kind."

They rode the rest of the way home in silence. And when the red light of the lamp shone out into the darkness of the cold and windy night, and he thought of this refuge for his children and wife, Haskins could have put his arm around the neck of his burly companion and squeezed him like a lover. But he contented himself with saying, "Steve Council, you'll git y'r pay f'r this some day."

"Don't want any pay. My religion ain't run on such business principles."

The wind was growing colder, and the ground was covered with a white frost, as they turned into the gate of the Council farm, and the children came rushing out, shouting, "Papa's come!" They hardly looked like the same children who had sat at the table the night before. Their torpidity, under the influence of sunshine and Mother Council, had given way to a sort of spasmodic cheerfulness, as insects in winter revive when laid on the hearth.

III

Haskins worked like a fiend, and his wife, like the heroic woman that she was, bore also uncomplainingly the most terrible burdens. They rose early and toiled without intermission till the darkness fell on the plain, then tumbled into bed, every bone and muscle aching with fatigue, to rise with the sun next morning to the same round of the same ferocity of labor.

The eldest boy drove a team all through the spring, ploughing and seeding, milked the cows, and did chores innumerable, in most ways taking the place of a man.

An infinitely pathetic but common figure — this boy on the American farm, where there is no law against child labor. To see him in his coarse clothing, his huge boots, and his ragged cap, as he staggered with a pail of water from the well, or trudged in the cold and cheerless dawn out into the frosty field behind his team, gave the city-bred visitor a sharp pang of sympathetic pain. Yet Haskins loved his boy, and would have saved him from this if he could, but he could not.

By June the first year the result of such Herculean toil began to show on the farm.

The yard was cleaned up and sown to grass, the garden ploughed and planted, and the house mended.

Council had given them four of his cows.

"Take 'em an' run 'em on shares. I don't want 'o milk s' many. Ike's away s' much now, Sat'd'ys an' Sund'ys, I can't stand the bother anyhow."

Other men, seeing the confidence of Council in the newcomer, had sold him tools on time; and as he was really an able farmer, he soon had round him many evidences of his care and thrift. At the advice of Council he had taken the farm for three years, with the privilege of re-renting or buying at the end of the term.

"It's a good bargain, an' y' want 'o nail it," said Council. "If you have any kind ov a crop, you c'n pay y'r debts, an' keep seed an' bread."

The new hope which now sprang up in the heart of Haskins and his wife grew great almost as a pain by the time the wide field of wheat began to wave and rustle and swirl in the winds of July. Day after day he would snatch a few moments after supper to go and look at it.

"Have ye seen the wheat t'-day, Nettie?" He asked one night as he rose from supper.

"No, Tim, I ain't had time."

"Well, take time now. Let's go look at it."

She threw an old hat on her head — Tommy's hat — and looking almost pretty in her thin, sad way, went out with her husband to the hedge.

"Ain't it grand, Nettie? Just look at it."

It was grand. Level, russet here and there, heavy-headed, wide as a lake, and full of multitudinous whispers and gleams of wealth, it stretched away before the gazers like the fabled field of the cloth of gold.

"Oh, I think — I hope we'll have a good

crop, Tim; and oh, how good the people have been to us!"

"Yes; I don't know where we'd be t'-day if it hadn't been f'r Council and his wife."

"They're the best people in the world," said the little woman, with a great sob of gratitude.

"We'll be in the field on Monday, sure," said Haskins, gripping the rail on the fence as if already at the work of the harvest.

The harvest came, bounteous, glorious, but the winds came and blew it into tangles, and the rain matted it here and there close to the ground, increasing the work of gathering it threefold.

Oh, how they toiled in those glorious days! Clothing dripping with sweat, arms aching, filled with briers, fingers raw and bleeding, backs broken with the weight of heavy bundles, Haskins and his man toiled on. Tommy drove the harvester, while his father and a hired man bound on the machine. In this way they cut ten acres every day, and almost every night after supper, when the hand went to bed, Haskins returned to the field shocking the bound grain in the light of the moon. Many a night he worked till his anxious wife came out at ten o'clock to call him in to rest and lunch.

At the same time she cooked for the men, took care of the children, washed and ironed, milked the cows at night, made the butter, and sometimes fed the horses and watered them while her husband kept at the shocking.

No slave in the Roman galleys could have toiled so frightfully and lived, for this man thought himself a free man, and that he was working for his wife and babes.

When he sank into his bed with a deep groan of relief, too tired to change his grimy, dripping clothing, he felt that he was getting nearer and nearer to a home of his own, and pushing the wolf of want a little farther from his door.

There is no despair so deep as the despair of a homeless man or woman. To roam the roads of the country or the streets of the city, to feel there is no rood of ground on which the feet can rest, to halt weary and hungry outside lighted windows and hear laughter and song within, — these are the hungers and rebellions that drive men to crime and women to shame.

It was the memory of this homelessness, and the fear of its coming again, that spurred Timothy Haskins and Nettie, his wife, to such ferocious labor during that first year.

IV

" 'M, yes; 'm, yes; first-rate," said Butler, as his eye took in the neat garden, the pigpen, and the well-filled barnyard. "You're gitt'n' quite a stook around yeh. Done well, eh?"

Haskins was showing Butler around the place. He had not seen it for a year, having spent the year in Washington and Boston with Ashley, his brother-in-law, who had been elected to Congress.

"Yes, I've laid out a good deal of money durin' the last three years. I've paid out three hundred dollars f'r fencin'."

"Um — h'm! I see, I see," said Butler, while Haskins went on:

"The kitchen there cost two hundred; the barn ain't cost much in money, but I've put a lot o' time on it. I've dug a new well, and I — "

"Yes, yes, I see. You've done well. Stock worth a thousand dollars," said Butler, picking his teeth with a straw.

"About that," said Haskins, modestly, "we begin to feel's if we was gitt'n' a home f'r ourselves; but we've worked hard. I tell you we begin to feel it, Mr. Butler, and we're goin' t' begin to ease up purty soon. We've been kind o' plannin' a trip back t' her folks after the fall ploughin's done."

"Eggs-actly!" said Butler, who was evidently thinking of something else. "I suppose you've kind o' calc'lated on stayin' here three years more?"

"Well, yes. Fact is, I think I c'n buy the farm this fall, if you'll give me a reasonable show."

"Um, — m! What do you call a reasonable show?"

"Well, say a quarter down and three years' time."

Butler looked at the huge stacks of wheat, which filled the yard, over which the chickens were fluttering and crawling, catching grasshoppers, and out of which the crickets were singing innumerably. He smiled in a peculiar way as he said, "Oh, I won't be hard on yeh. But what did you expect to pay f'r the place?"

"Why, about what you offered it for before, two thousand five hundred, or possibly three thousand dollars, he added quickly, as he saw the owner shake his head.

"This farm is worth five thousand and five hundred dollars," said Butler, in a careless and decided voice.

"What!" almost shrieked the astounded Haskins. "What's that? Five thousand? Why, that's double what you offered it for three years ago."

"Of course, and it's worth it. It was all run down then; now it's in good shape. You've laid out fifteen hundred dollars in improvements, according to your own story."

"But you had nothin' t' do about that. It's my work an' my money."

"You bet it was; but it's my land."

"But what's to pay me for all my — "

"Ain't you had the use of 'em?" replied Butler, smiling calmly into his face.

Haskins was like a man struck on the head with a sandbag; he couldn't think; he stammered as he tried to say: "But — I never'd git the use — You'd rob me! More 'n that: you agreed — you promised that I could buy or rent at the end of three years at — "

"That's all right. But I didn't say I'd let you carry off the improvements, nor that I'd go on renting the farm at two-fifty. The land is doubled in value, it don't matter how; it don't enter into the question; an' now you can pay me five hundred dollars a year rent, or take it on your own terms at fifty-five hundred, or — git out."

He was turning away when Haskins, the sweat pouring from his face, fronted him, saying again:

"But you've done nothing to make it so. You hain't added a cent. I put it all there myself, expectin' to buy. I worked an' sweat to improve it. I was workin' for myself an' babes — "

"Well, why didn't you buy when I offered to sell? What y' kickin' about?"

"I'm kickin' about payin' you twice f'r my own things, — my own fences, my own kitchen, my own garden."

Butler laughed. "You're too green t' eat, young feller. Your improvements! The law will sing another tune."

"But I trusted your word."

"Never trust anybody, my friend. Besides, I didn't promise not to do this thing. Why, man, don't look at me like that. Don't take me for a thief. It's the law. The reg'lar thing. Everybody does it."

"I don't care if they do. It's stealin' jest the same. You take three thousand dollars of my money — the work o' my hands and my wife's." He broke down at this point. He was not a strong man mentally. He could face hardship, ceaseless toil, but he could not face the cold and sneering face of Butler.

"But I don't take it," said Butler, coolly. "All you've got to do is to go on jest as you've been a-doin', or give me a thousand dollars down, and a mortgage at ten per cent on the rest.

Haskins sat down blindly on a bundle of oats near by, and with staring eyes and drooping head went over the situation. He was under the lion's paw. He felt a horrible numbness in his heart and limbs. He was hid in a mist, and there was no path out.

Butler walked about, looking at the huge stacks of grain, and pulling now and again a few handfuls out, shelling the heads in his hands and blowing the chaff away. He hummed a little tune as he did so. He had an accommodating air of waiting.

Haskins was in the midst of the terrible toil of the last year. He was walking again in the rain and the mud behind his plough; he felt the dust and dirt of the threshing. The ferocious husking-time, with its cutting wind and biting, clinging snows, lay hard upon him. Then he thought of his wife, how she had cheerfully cooked and baked, without holiday and without rest.

"Well, what do you think of it?" inquired the cool, mocking insinuating voice of Butler.

"I think you're a thief and a liar!"

shouted Haskins, leaping up. "A black-hearted houn'!" Butler's smile maddened him; with a sudden leap he caught a fork in his hand, and whirled it in the air. "You'll never rob another man, damn ye!" he grated through his teeth, a look of pitiless ferocity in his accusing eyes.

Butler shrank and quivered, expecting the blow; stood, held hypnotized by the eyes of the man he had a moment before despised — a man transformed into an avenging demon. But in the deadly hush between the lift of the weapon and its fall there came a gush of faint, childish laughter and then across the range of his vision, far away and dim, he saw the sun-bright head of his baby girl, as with the pretty, tottering run of a two-year-old, she moved across the grass of the door-yard. His hands relaxed; the fork fell to the ground; his head lowered.

"Make out y'r deed an' mor'gage, an' git off'n my land, an' don't ye never cross my line agin; if y' do, I'll kill ye."

Butler backed away from the man in wild haste, and climbing into his buggy with trembling limbs drove off down the road, leaving Haskins seated dumbly on the sunny pile of sheaves, his head sunk into his hands.

Washington Gladden: THE EMBATTLED FARMERS

THE farmers of the United States are up in arms. They are the bone and sinew of the nation; they produce the largest share of its wealth; but they are getting, they say, the smallest share for themselves. The American farmer is steadily losing ground. His burdens are heavier every year and his gains are more meager; he is beginning to fear that he may be sinking into a servile condition. He has waited long for the redress of his grievances; he purposes to wait no longer.

Washington Gladden, "The Embattled Farmers," *Forum*, X (November 1890), 315–322.

Whatever he can do by social combinations, or by united political action, to remove the disabilities under which he is suffering, he intends to do at once and with all his might. There is no doubt at all that the farmers of this country are tremendously in earnest just now, and they have reason to be. Beyond question they are suffering sorely. The business of farming has become, for some reasons, extremely unprofitable. With the hardest work and with the sharpest economy, the average farmer is unable to make both ends meet; every year closes with debt, and the mortgage grows till it devours the land. The labor bureau of Connecticut has shown, by an investigation of 693 representative farms, that the average annual reward of the farm proprietor of that State, for his expenditure of muscle and brain, is $181.31, while the average annual wages of the ordinary hired man is $386.36. Even if the price of board must come out of the hired man's stipend, it still leaves him a long way ahead of his employer. In Massachusetts the case is a little better; the average farmer makes $326.49, while his hired man gets $345.

In a fertile district in the State of New York, a few weeks ago, an absentee landlord advertised for a man to manage his farm. The remuneration offered was not princely. The farm manager was to have his rent, his garden, pasturage for one cow, and a salary of $250 a year, for his services and those of his wife. There was a rush of applicants for the place. Who were they? Many of them were capable and intelligent farmers who had lost their own farms in the hopeless struggle with adverse conditions, and who were now well content to exchange their labor and their experience against a yearly reward of $250. The instance is typical. Throughout the eastern States, with the home market which protection is supposed to have built up at their very doors, the farmers are falling behind. Says Professor C. S. Walker:

"A careful study of New England farming in the light of all points of view, carried on for the past ten years by means of statistical investigation, personal observation during carriage drives from Canada to Long Island Sound, and intimate association with all classes of farmers, assures one that the man who cultivates an average farm and depends upon its profits alone for the support of himself and family, if he pay his taxes and debts, cannot compete with his brothers, or attain to their standard of living, who, with equal powers, employ them in other walks of life."

The same story is heard in the central States. In Ohio farms are offered for beggarly rents, and even on these favorable terms farming does not pay. Tenant farmers are throwing up their leases and moving into the cities, well content to receive as common laborers a dollar and a quarter a day, and to pay such rents and to run such risks of enforced idleness as the change involves. In the South the case is even worse. Under a heavy burden of debt the farmer struggles on from year to year, the phenomenal growth of the manufacturing interests in his section seeming to bring him but slight relief. And even in the West we find the same state of things. A large share of recent corn crops has been consumed for fuel; and over vast areas, Mr. C. Wood Davis tells us, "wheat sells at from 40 to 50 cents, oats at from 9 to 12 cents, and corn at from 10 to 13 cents a bushel, and fat cattle at from 1½ to 3 cents a pound." Under such conditions the life of the western farmer cannot be prosperous. From Kansas and Nebraska and Dakota the cry is no less loud and bitter than from Connecticut and New York and North Carolina.

The causes of this lamentable state of things are many. Who shall estimate them? Mr. Davis gives this list: "Monometallism, deficient or defective circulating medium, protective tariffs, trusts, dressed-beef combinations, speculation in farm products, over-greedy middlemen, and exorbitant transportation rates." These are a few of the disadvantages of which the farmers now complain. Doubtless several of these causes are working against them. Whether, in their diagnosis of the disease, they always put their finger on the right spot, may be doubted. People cannot always be trusted to tell what ails them. The patient knows that he is suffering, but he does not always discover the nature of his malady. Mr. Davis gives strong reasons for the belief that the root of the difficulty is over-production; that there are too many farms, and that more corn, wheat, oats, beef, and pork have been raised than the country can use. There is the foreign market, to be sure; but in that the farmer of the West must compete with the low-priced labor of India and of Russia. If his product is very greatly in excess of the wants of his own country, he will be forced to sell at very low prices. The fact seems to be that the less of these staples the farmers raise, the more they get for them. The short crops of this year may, very likely, bring them more money than the enormous crops of 1889. The comforting assurance of Mr. Davis, that the acreage of farms cannot increase so rapidly in the future, and that the population will soon grow up to the food supply and will redress the balance in the farmer's favor, is one that may well be cherished.

But granting that this is the chief cause of the depression of agriculture, other causes of considerable importance should not be overlooked. The enormous tribute which the farmers of the West are paying to the money-lenders of the East, is one source of their poverty. Scarcely a week passes that does not bring to me circulars from banking firms and investment agencies all over the West begging for money to be loaned on farms at eight or nine per cent. net. The cost of negotiation and collection, which the farmer must pay, considerably increases these rates. The descriptive lists of farms which accompany these circulars show that the mortgages are not all given for purchase money. I find in one of the agricultural papers the following figures indicating the increase in farm mortgages in Dane County, Wisconsin, during the year 1889. The number of mortgages filed was 467; the average amount of each, $1,252; the total amount, $584,727.80; the number of mortgages given for purchase money, only nine. But whether the mortgages represent debts incurred in the purchase of the land or those incurred for other purposes, it is evident that when they bear such rates of interest they constitute a burden under which no kind of business can be profitably carried on. The farmer who voluntarily pays such tribute as this to the money-lenders is quite too sanguine. Other business men will not handicap themselves in this way. But probably the larger proportion of these mortgages are extorted from the farmers by hard necessity. Not their hope of increased prosperity makes them incur these debts so often as the pressure of obligations which have been incurred and which must be met.

The steady and increasing migration from the farms to the cities, is in part an effect of the depression of agriculture and in part a cause of that depression. If a large part of the most vigorous and enterprising members of the farmers' families leave the farms, it is evident that the farms will not be carried on with the enterprise and vigor which are necessary to the success of any business. Is it not true that less ingenuity and less invention have been developed in this business than in most other occupations? There is plenty of money in the country; might not the farmer, by the application of brains to his calling, get a little more of it? Of the great staples, the country can consume only a limited quantity; but the country is ready to take all sorts of fancy food products — delicacies, luxuries, gastronomic novelties — and to pay good prices for them. A few years ago, Mr. Gladstone, speaking to the farmers in a Scotch district where agriculture was greatly depressed, asked them why they did not try the production of jam for the city markets. He pointed out that the small fruits from which this luxury could be compounded would grow well in their soil, and that for such articles there was always a good market. The Tory editors laughed at Mr. Gladstone's kitchen economy, but the Scotch farmers took the matter seriously and have found profit in it. A large and productive industry has sprung from the old statesman's suggestion. Along some such lines as these the farmers will most surely draw to themselves a larger share of the surplus wealth of the country. That surplus is abundant, but all sorts of people with keen wits and strenuous energies are competing for it. Those who have it are ready to exchange it for gratifications of various sorts. The problem is to please them. Within the bounds of innocent and wholesome delectation there is a wide range for the exercise of invention by the food-producers of the nation. If they confine themselves to the business of raising corn and wheat and pork and beef, their market will be narrow. They can widen it almost indefinitely if they will devote to their business the same kind of ingenuity that manufacturers of all classes are

constantly exercising in their efforts to attract to their own coffers the abundance of the land.

Such methods, however, are not those by which the farmers now hope to better their condition. They are organized mainly for other purposes. They believe that the miseries under which they are suffering are largely due to political causes and can be cured by legislation. They have found out that of the twenty millions of bread-winners they comprise eight or nine millions, and they think that if they stand together they can get such legislation as they desire. The old Grange kept pretty well out of politics; the new Farmers' Alliance and its affiliated organizations intend to work the political placer for all that it can be made to yield. Hear them:

"The prime object of this association is to better the condition of the farmers of America, mentally, morally, and financially, to suppress personal, sectional, and national prejudices, all unhealthful rivalry and selfish ambition; to return to the principles on which the government was founded, by adhering to the doctrine of equal rights, and equal chances to all and special privileges to none; to educate and commingle with those of the same calling, to the end that country life may become less lonely and more social; to assist the weak with the strength of the strong, thereby rendering the whole body more able to resist; and to bequeath to posterity conditions that will enable them, as honest, intelligent, industrious producers, to cope successfully with the exploiting class of middlemen."

For the promotion of these objects three methods are named — "social, business, and political." The social feature is easily understood; the business methods involve various forms of cooperative buying and selling; and the political methods are defined only by saying that they are strictly non-partisan, and that they must ever remain so. This seems to mean that the farmers decline to attach themselves to either political party, but that they will try to make both parties serve them.

"All questions in political economy will be thoroughly discussed, and when the order can agree on a reform as necessary, they will demand it of the government and of every political party; and if the demand goes unheeded, they will find ways to enforce it. The most essential reforms must come from legislation, but that does not necessarily compel the necessity of choosing candidates and of filling the offices. Such a course may become necessary, but it will not be resorted to under any other circumstances."

This is pretty explicit, and it is beginning to exert a solemnizing influence in the councils of the politicians. The Farmers' Alliance is not unconscious of its power. The movement is running like wild-fire over all our hills and prairies, and it is claimed that forty members of the next Congress will be pledged to support its demands. What will be its demands?

I. Cheap money, to begin with. The farmers are generally debtors; they want cheap money wherewith to pay their debts. Of course the cheaper the money, the less groceries and clothing and machinery can be bought with it; but the farmers think of their debts more than of their necessities, and the longing of their souls is for cheap money. They are therefore in favor of the free coinage of silver; but they insist that even this would be an ineffectual remedy, since only about $45,000,000 a year, at the utmost, could thus be added to the currency of the country, and this amount, they think, would be ridiculously inadequate.

II. The sub-treasury plan, so called, by which warehouses are to be built in every county where they are demanded, wherein the farmers may deposit cotton, wheat, corn, oats, or tobacco, receiving in return a treasury note for 80 per cent of the value of the product so deposited, at the current market price. These treasury notes are to be legal tender for debts and receivable for customs. A warehouse receipt, also, is to be given to the depositor, designating the amount and grade of the product deposited and the amount of money advanced upon it, and indicating that interest upon the money thus advanced is to be paid by the depositor at the rate of one per cent. per annum. These receipts are to be negotiable by indorsement. The holder of a receipt, by presenting it at the warehouse, returning the money advanced, and paying interest and charges, may obtain the product deposited; and the money thus returned is to be destroyed by the Secretary of the Treasury. This scheme for getting an ample supply of money directly into the hands of the farmers, at a nominal rate of interest, appears to have the indorsement of the Alliance. The journals of the organization are discussing it freely, and are adducing various historical instances to show that the principle involved in it has been tested and found valid; but the verdict of most economists and financiers is strongly against the measure.

III. The ownership by the government of all the railroads, telegraphs, and telephones, is another plank in the platform of the Alliance. Here is a measure which is certainly debatable; let us hope that the farmers will secure for it a thorough discussion.

IV. The prohibition of gambling in stocks and that of alien ownership of land, are propositions which will also receive considerable support outside the Alliance.

V. The abolition of national banks and

the substitution of legal-tender treasury notes for national-bank notes, will not, probably, command universal assent.

VI. The adoption of a constitutional amendment requiring the choice of United States senators by the people, seems to be a popular measure among the members of the Alliance. To this they will be able to rally a strong support.

With these and other demands inscribed upon their banners, the farmers are in the field. They will make lively work for the politicians in the West and in the South during the pending campaign. No small amount of dodging and ducking on the part of these worthies may be looked for. Several of the strong agricultural districts will return to Congress men pledged to advocate the measures of the Alliance. Already they have picked out the place which they wish their contingent to occupy on either side of the center aisle in the House of Representatives, where they expect to hold the balance of power, and to take the place of the Center in the French Assembly.

How long they will hold together is difficult to predict. It may be that the discussions in which they must take part will show them that some of the measures of direct relief on which they are chiefly depending are impracticable; and it is conceivable that this discovery will tend to demoralize them. That they can become a permanent political force is not likely, for parties which represent only classes cannot live in a republic. But several results, by no means undesirable, may be looked for as the outcome of this farmers' uprising.

1. They will secure a thorough discussion of some important economical questions. They will force the people to consider carefully the problem of the state ownership of the great public highways. It is not absurd to demand that the state should own and control, even if it does not operate, the railroads; and that it should own and operate the telegraphs. The conclusion to which such an experienced railway manager as the president of the Chicago and Alton Railway has already come, is one to which many other people are likely to come in the course of this debate. If the farmers can stick together, and can stick to their text long enough to get this business thoroughly ventilated, they will do a good service. 2. They are loosening the bands of partisanship and are opening the way for a rational co-operation of citizens for all desirable purposes. "The most hopeful feature of this whole uprising," writes a shrewd observer, "is the smashing of the old party shackles that goes along with it." That it may lead to a reconstruction of parties, is not improbable. 3. They are helping to make an end of the sectionalism which has been a large part of the capital of a certain class of politicians. Their manifestoes point to this as the one striking result of their work thus far. "Scarcely a vestige," they say, "of the old sectional prejudice of a few years ago is now visible within our ranks." The South and the West are coming into fraternal relations. Mr. Lodge has already discovered that the West is not supporting his Force Bill. "The demagogue politician who now attempts to array sectional prejudice in order that he may keep farmers equally divided on important questions," is admonished that he is about to confront "a superior intelligence that will soon convince him that his occupation is gone."

The farmers' movement is not, probably, the deluge; but it will prove to be something of a shower — in some quarters a cyclone — and it will clear the atmosphere.

J. Laurence Laughlin:

CAUSES OF AGRICULTURAL UNREST

A TRAVELER following the path of La Salle across the plains of the Illinois to-day would be struck, even on the most superficial survey, by the signs of agricultural prosperity. Broad farms, substantial buildings, bursting cribs, fields drained with tile, and every evidence of good farming are visible. The original settlers, moreover, have won their fortunes and retired to the neighboring towns to spend their years of rest. It is common to find men who have amassed, from farming, fortunes counted by hundreds of thousands of dollars. Iowa, also, is certainly to-day a successful farming community. And wherever a man of executive ability and training in farming has taken up agriculture upon a good soil, there comfort and prosperity are pretty sure to be found. But there is another side to the picture. A fire lies somewhere below all this Populistic smoke which has risen from the granger agitation and rolled ominously over the skies from Chicago and St. Louis during the past summer.

Behind the political evolutions of the parties which have marshaled themselves under the leadership of Mr. Bryan there have been some forces at work which it may be interesting to record. The fact that so many delusions could result in a kind of political unity, and could produce common political action, itself demands explanation. In truth, the earnestness of great groups of fanatical men in the Chicago convention has even a touch of pathos about it, the more that they are evidently sincere and honest. They represent, however, certain strata in our economic and social organization. Throughout the newer States we find a widely spread class of undereducated, brawny, earnest, but narrow minds. There is little pliability in their mental processes. Once the single-idead brain has been occupied by a theory, or craze, the gate to all other ideas is thereby closed. In a brain incapable of economic and judicial reasoning, the one idea now in possession engenders prejudice, and even, in an emotional nature, frenzy. This class of minds may not always have the same craze, but, in its undereducated way, it is sure to have one of some sort. The subject of the fanaticism may change in time, but with the fanaticism we must always reckon so long as the undereducated class exists and wields a large political power.

The honest but narrow mind is ever the prey of knaves. The cheat plies his trade among the untrained so long as the eternal-gullible maintains its seat in the human heart. The shiftless incapable purposely frames a scheme to make something out of nothing, which often appeals to the naive honest as the cloud of fire by night guiding them out of the desert. Thus two general classes, both hoping to acquire riches by legerdemain, by tricks of legislation, come to work together for a common aim. The honesty of the one is the mask for the dishonesty of the other; and they are stimulated, in the attempt

James Laurence Laughlin, "Causes of Agricultural Unrest," *Atlantic Monthly,* 78 (November, 1896), 577–585.

to rub the lamp of fortune for the sake of obtaining sudden riches without the sweat of the brow, by the picture, familiar to us in the rapid development of a young country rich in varied resources, of men of their own undereducated kind who have stumbled upon great wealth. The man who for years has been eating his bacon over a deposit of petroleum, coal, copper, or gold, awakes some day to great wealth, puts on the fine linen of civilization, and stands as the possibility of what may at any moment come to every other one of his kind. Cupidity nudges the elbow of fanaticism. While this human quality is not confined to any particular part of our country, yet in the newer States there is an energetic restlessness in urging a peculiar nostrum to which the older part of the country is a stranger.

The narrow mind — like a popgun in which the last wad shoots out the first — honestly holds to its one idea, but this idea is driven out by any new agitation strong enough to force in another idea which may displace the old. The basis of the old greenback delusion, following the commercial crisis of 1873, was this same mental quality. The optimism of the Western spirit has created cities like Chicago, and it even built the palaces of the White City, but in feeble intellects this optimism is the spring to many harmful kinds of activity. In its expansive way it sees results before they have gone through the formality of taking place. The mere possibility of borrowing is itself almost the realization of brilliant dreams. The possession of a loan is a ladder to the pinnacle of life. The return of the loan to the lender and the way down the ladder again find no place in the imagination of the borrower.

Such is the background of my picture. We can see the characteristics out of which a certain kind of results will surely come. The greenback craze was the outcome of a depression following a long period of extraordinary inflation and speculation after the Civil War. When the bubble burst in 1873, business disasters were not confined to the farming class. Expansion of trade, inflated prices, airy ventures of all kinds collapsed, and brought down men of affairs in every occupation with pitiless impartiality. The farmer, having entered into engagements for large sums when all the world was booming with speculative schemes of development, suddenly found himself prone on the ground, with his flying-machine lying splintered and ruined beside him. But in this fate he found himself in company with men engaged in all branches of manufacture and trade. It is in such a soil, composed of the débris of speculation and over-trading, that a crop of weedy delusions grows. It is commonly known that the years succeeding a panic are the ones in which quack remedies for industrial distress find many gullible victims. Untrained in economic reasoning, inexperienced in industrial history, untaught in penetrating into the causes of commercial phenomena, the undereducated man is the prey to the first nostrum that happens to be offered him. His distress pinches. How easy to believe the dogmatic assertion that the cause of his distress is the "scarcity of money"! Why not? He knows precious little about the principles of money. Why should it not be that, as well as something else of which he knows equally little? It is all mysterious, anyway. He must believe the statements of the man who first gets his confidence. Therefore, in times of industrial depression we have always had an epidemic of crazes. We know that in many former depressions the remedies proposed have had nothing whatever to do with silver, which to-day appears as the sovereign cure. In 1874 it was a greenback wad in the popgun; since then the silver wad has driven out the greenback wad. In both cases it was clear that industrial disaster was due to trading beyond all reason and judgment, and that the quantity of money did not determine the quantity of goods and property in existence.

Of course, the farmer who has over-traded, or expanded his operations beyond his means, in a time of commercial depression is affected just as any one else is in like conditions. After 1873 he probably found himself in goodly company, but the present difficulties seem to be limited to farming. It is quite certain that in the last few years special conditions have surrounded the farmer and placed him in a peculiar position, — conditions which have not been common to men in other industries. If a period of over-development, confined almost entirely to agricultural interests, has been followed by the inevitable reaction, we may expect to see all the evidences of distress in rural communities which follow in the wake of a general commercial crisis; and we may expect to find also that nostrum-mongers have come to the fore, charming and deluding the honestly distressed farmer with the magic of their patent remedies. It boots nothing that the diagnosis is wrong or that the medicine is unfit; the mind of one idea, by its nature, is hospitable to the first-comer, and prejudice closes the door to the advice of the trained physician who arrives later.

In the genuine Populistic programme silver plays but an unimportant role. For political purposes, it is skillfully made the common basis of action, in this campaign, by different groups of persons. Yet it is less hungrily demanded than inconvertible paper, or the sub-treasury scheme, or the income tax, or greater freedom from the militia, by the mind of the true Populist. In short, the conditions of agriculture have permitted the growth of numerous crazes, of which silver is not even the tallest weed in the soil. Behind silver lies a whole thistle crop of ideas, with which we must eventually deal. We shall have to face various schemes of redistribution of property, even after the silver question has gone to its long home with the greenback. A craze is the inevitable manifestation of an idea strongly held by under-educated men. If it is not the greenback craze or the silver craze, it will be some other.

While understanding that vagaries are prolific in a season of financial distress, the essence of our inquiry is to discover the causes which have brought about this situation of hardship. To one who has watched the larger industrial movements of recent decades it is clear that very powerful currents have been set in motion, the force and direction of which may be unknown to the very persons who are unconsciously carried along on their surface. In this study, it may be possible, so to speak, to cast some sealed bottles into the currents, and thereby record their trend and force.

We are now witnessing in practical operation in the United States a difficult adjustment of the farming industry under an economic principle as old as Ricardo. If only for geographical reasons, the new-comers to an unsettled country originally plant themselves upon the soil most conveniently situated to harbors and rivers, irrespective of the fact that soil much richer and more fertile lies in the interior. The poorer soil accessible to transportation is, in fact, the richer soil to the settler, who is saved the sacrifices of location distant from the market. So long as water furnished the arteries of transportation and trade, settlements were placed upon seacoasts and rivers. Rich farming communities spread over the outlying districts adjacent to these settlements. The thin soil of New England once masqueraded in the guise of a prosperous farming district, but that is now a thing of the past. And when Mr. Whittier, in the pages of this magazine, mourned the decay of the farm and of rural life, and the departure of the ambitious boy to the town or city, he touched with song the hard facts of an economic revolution.

The same pitiless wave which has swept over Great Britain in recent decades, spreading confusion and disaster in English farming, reducing prices of farm products, shriveling English rent-rolls, changing the character of agriculture in many districts, has spread its influence also over New England and the rest of the Eastern States, — a wave set in motion by the progress of the age, by the railway and the improved steamship. Its immediate effect was to bring the products of new, distant, and vastly richer farming-land into the same markets where the products of the old and poorer soil had been sold. In economic phrase, it was the insertion, into existing grades of cultivated land, of new grades of higher fertility. Consequently, if the required supply of food can now be produced more cheaply by the new and better soils, the old grades must go out of cultivation. It mattered not, in the inevitable onward sweep of this evolution of the fittest instrument of production, — bringing cheaper food to hungry legions, — that the owner of the old farm had attachments of heart and association to the old lanes, the old blue hills, and the old trees. The progress of the age was under it all, like a ploughshare upturning the nest of his youth.

The railway and the steamship have not yet ceased their iconoclastic operations. A few years ago, the varied expanses of middle New York and the broad valleys of the Susquehanna made up the flower of our farms and gave solid incomes to their owners. This state of things is now of the past. Farming is no longer profitable in these districts, because more fertile though distant lands have been brought within reach of markets. The richer wheat-land in the middle West, and of the prairies of Minnesota and Dakota, lay untouched until the railway opened up a cheaper transportation to the lakes and seaboard. The cause of the enforced agricultural readjustment in the United States was the progress of the age, represented mainly by the modern railway. The fall of railway rates to less than one cent per ton per mile, and the generally dubious condition of railway securities as investments, are glaring evidences of the pressure to secure cheap transportation in the exploitation of the West.

It is a strange development — indeed, a curious travesty on justice — that the railway, which by reason of its low cost of transportation has practically destroyed the farming interests of the East, should be regarded by the farmer of the West as the vampire sucking out the blood of his agricultural profits; and yet the Western lands could have been opened to seaboard markets only by means of it and its low rates. The Eastern farmer must justly regard the railway, and the resultant competition of the richer farm-land in the West, as the cause of his ruin and the force which has driven him to new employments; the Western farmer would not now be in existence if it were not for the railway. The proof that it has served the Western farmer well is to be found in the sad ruins of Eastern agriculture. But by such revolutions is the progress of invention marked. Every great improvement which has cheapened the cost of reproducing existing forms of capital has necessarily lowered the value of that previously made, to the level at which it can be reproduced. Ocean steamships which cost $500,000 each five years ago — and which could now be built for $400,000 — must have fallen in their capitalized value by one fifth, or twenty per cent, irrespective of depreciation by wear and tear. In a similar way, the general introduction of steamships has lowered the selling price of sailing vessels. Every owner of capital in its various forms must always take the risk that invention may devise something cheaper in operation than his existing machinery.

By the nature of his occupation, a farmer is subject to this principle quite as much as any owner of capital. His land may for the moment be the best in cultivation for wheat; but any conceivable discovery, or any improvement of existing devices, by which, directly or indirectly, new soils in any part of the world may be brought into competition with his own, must lower the price of his farm products. The wheat-growing farmer is, therefore, at the mercy of world-causes, and not merely of the domestic events within the boundaries of his own country. The reason is that wheat is a commodity whose price is not determined by home, but by foreign markets. We ourselves do not consume nearly the whole product of our wheat or cotton land. We export largely beyond our own consumption. We exported in 1892 — a good year — 157,280,351 bushels of wheat, and 15,-196,769 barrels of wheat flour, when our total yield of wheat was 515,949,000 bushels. It will at once appear to the reader how surely the price of wheat must respond to influences quite out of the ken of the ordinary farmer, and yet that the continuance of farming depends upon his

keeping careful watch of all the forces affecting his business, wherever and however they may be acting throughout the world.

The simple facts that we produce more wheat than we consume, and that, consequently, the price of the whole crop is determined, not by the markets within this country, but by the world-markets, are sufficient to put wheat, as regards its price, in a different class from those articles whose markets are local. It differs very radically, for example, from corn: while we export 36.88 per cent of our wheat crop, we export only 3.72 per cent of our corn crop (which in 1892 was 1,628,464,000 bushels). Whether he knows it or not, whether he likes it or not, every man who chooses as his occupation in life the growing of wheat must be affected by everything which influences the production and price of that article throughout the entire world. And it need not be said that many wheat-growing farmers make little or no allowance for events beyond the limited range of local information. A good crop in Europe means a lessened demand for American wheat; a large European crop, accompanied by a very large harvest at home, is sure to depress the price abnormally; and if, in addition to these two uniting causes, competing countries in Asia, South America, Africa, and Australia send large quantities of the same grain to Europe, the price may fall still further. A given demand may be more than met by an exceptional supply. It must then be remembered, too, that as regards an article of food like wheat, after a person has taken his usual quantity, his demand does not rise with a falling price, but, after a saturation point of desire is reached, it practically ceases altogether. This accounts for the extreme fall in price produced by a supply only slightly in excess of the ordinary demand. Does the farmer of our Western States study to adapt his supply to the known demand, as the manufacturer does? Probably not: he plants because he has wheat-land, and leaves the rest to the mysterious play of forces outside his ken. Yet it is certain, nevertheless, that the price of his grain is determined by events in Australia, Argentina, Egypt, India, Hungary, and Russia, or by excessive rains in England, France, or Germany. To know the economic nature of the farmer's occupation is necessary to an understanding of his existing situation, and one can clearly see how varied are the world-influences which may affect his efforts in growing wheat.

The revolution by which invention and progress have forced a readjustment of industries, with a better relation to our natural resources, has wrenched the country and twisted it into new shapes. It has taken away the farming industry from the older States, and given it to the newer territory where soils are richer. The problem left to the farmers of the Middle States is the difficult problem correctly to learn the causes of the agricultural readjustment; to master the qualities of the old soil for other crops; scientifically to adapt the land to the new conditions brought by the opening up of new areas of superior soil. It is a problem requiring a high order of intelligence and scientific training in farming.

But a problem which under the most favorable conditions would be a complex and difficult one, is made far more serious by a movement which has taken away from farming the most enterprising spirits and the most vigorous brains. The movement of the better minds away from the farms to the towns, where a wider career is opened, is so well known to Americans that I do not need to describe it. Enterprising spirits have left New England

mainly to the small farming of the Irish; and the Middle States have likewise enlarged their quotas in the towns. It is one of the most marked events in our economic history. The brightest youths speed to the cities as a matter of course.

But even if, with Mr. Whittier, we sing dolorously of the abandoned farm, we cannot fail to see above the horizon the expanding roofs of the manufacturing town and the glittering attractions of the greater cities. We must see also a larger power to purchase food and other necessaries in the wages of the daily laborer, graded schools instead of the "district" schools, better drainage, better lighting, a larger nervous excitement, more stimulus to the plodding mind, a response to the offer of more intellectual tonics, a wider reading, and a more intelligent acquaintance with the lives and manners of cultivated persons. If the moral tone of the city and town be low, in all probability children there are safer than on the farm, from vulgar vice, and from that inward moral starvation which follows upon a lack of mental nourishment. In short, when in some farming districts one notes the bad roads, the social privation, the lonely isolation of farm life, one wonders that there are any farmers. The movement to the towns is really in answer to a craving for something besides mere material existence; it arises from a delight in the society of others and in access to books and information; from aesthetic satisfaction and a general striving for the better thing.

The effect of these revolutions upon farming was that in those years when a great industrial readjustment was taking place which required the best efforts of the best intelligences, at the very time when the hardest problem was presented for solution, social forces were at work to take away the men best capable of solving the problem. Just as the situation became more serious, the least efficient were left to meet it. It is not necessary for me to say, by way of qualification, that there are efficient farmers; of course there are. Wherever one finds executive ability and training in farming, there one is likely to see success, as in any other occupation of life. But I wish to emphasize my general point, that from the nature of his occupation the farmer is subjected to world-wide operations requiring careful foresight; that the age is bringing him new adjustments and new problems; and yet that the concomitant part of the situation has been a marked reduction, due to the attractions of our cities, in the quality of farming skill and capacity.

But the farmers on the richer soils of the trans-Mississippi States, although holding the coigne of vantage relatively to other farmers in this country, especially as regards wheat-growing, have been themselves affected by special influences of an unfavorable kind. In the years of prosperity after recovery from the panic of 1873, the Western farming districts witnessed a curious epidemic of loans, an unexampled prevalence of borrowing-made-easy. Eastern money-lenders sent unlimited sums, with reckless confidence, to be loaned on Western farm mortgages. So little discrimination was exercised in this expansive era that the droughty lands of Kansas and Nebraska were estimated to be as good security as the more trustworthy soil of Iowa and Minnesota. Methods of lending were careless; and the unwary met sad treatment at the hands of rogues, or fell victims to poor land-titles. The abundance of loanable capital was a premium on borrowing, and few farmers in need of improving their farms escaped the temptation. They were led into plans for expenditure without fully realizing the risks of farming, the

operation of world-causes upon agricultural prices, or the difficulties of repaying loans after they were spent.

Following the recovery from the panic of 1873, the development of western Minnesota and Dakota reached a stage of speculative expansion quite as dashing and bold as any ventures of Wall Street brokers. Over-confidence was sublime. No other part of the country was comparable for sound investment to this wheat Eldorado; the East was a doubtful place for solid prosperity in comparison with this brilliant addition to our resources. Fortunes were to be made only in farming. Fathers bought shares in the ventures undertaken by their sons who had moved to the new West. Old residents of Ohio, Illinois, or Wisconsin sold their lands to join the great hegira. In its way it was as picturesque and exciting as any like event in our history; and it would not be easy to exaggerate the intensity of this period of the early eighties, soon after the resumption of specie payments.

This over-development was to the farmers what overtrading is to the commercial world. The expansion having gone beyond legitimate bounds, the reaction was certain to come. The drought, hot winds, and consequent failure of crops, in Kansas and Nebraska, startled Eastern lenders into the discovery that the lands were in many cases valueless as security. The time for repayment of loans came around, and brought with it a test of the good judgment of the borrowers in the use of their loans. Bad judgment and lack of skill meant inability to repay. "Settling day" is in any market a solemn occasion, but in the case of farm loans it is sure to reveal all the weak spots. A vast deal of capital, of course, was properly lent, and wisely expended in improvements; but this was far from being commonly true. In justification of this statement I need do no more than refer to the recent failures of Western mortgage companies, and to the present generally suspicious attitude in regard to their investments. I do not imply, by any means, that there are not good Western farm mortgages, but only that the era of speculation has been followed by the inevitable reaction.

Under the influence of this period farmers had borrowed, and pledged themselves to the payment of fixed units of money. While agriculture was booming, the ability to change wheat into these units for repayment seemed easy; and if this situation had remained unchanged all might have gone well. But there soon came a heaving of the calm sea, showing that storms were going on in other parts of the wide waters. As I have pointed out, world-causes must be taken into account. Just when the reaction in American farming began to set in, the distant countries of the world, which had begun to send wheat to the same competitive markets, rapidly increased their exports. The sudden enlargement of the supply without any corresponding increase in demand produced that alarming fall in the price of wheat which has been made the farmer's excuse for thinking that silver is the magic panacea for all his ills. At the very time when the American farmer was under pressure to increase his production in every possible way, he was disastrously affected by a similar increase in other countries. In short, the agencies which opened up the superior wheat-fields of the Dakotas have not been confined to the United States. The progress of the age in the form of cheapened railway transportation revolutionized the agriculture of our country; but likewise the progress of the age in the form of cheapened steamship transportation opened up to European consumers the superior wheat-fields of Argentina, Australia, Egypt, and India. Yet the Western farmer ploughed and sowed blindly, as if his were the only sources of wheat supply in the world.

Here is the pith of the whole trouble of the farmer of the farther West. A boom and wild expansion consequent upon the settlement of the Dakotas brought about the inevitable reaction. The one serious difficulty to the sufferer was that there were special conditions, in a great measure influencing agriculture alone, which produced the same results that a violent commercial crisis produces in a wide range of industries. To be sure, a disaster in farming conveys the impact of damage to other allied interests; but here were conditions, the results of seismic convulsions throughout the world, practically uncomprehended by those most deeply affected, and yet not directly touching other great industries. Developments special to agriculture, although radiating all over the world, narrowed in upon our Western farmers, quite unconscious of the currents that were bearing them up and dashing them on the rocks. If we understand, then, that the agriculture of the middle West has been suffering bitterly from readjustment; and more than this, that even the favored farmers of the richest land in the remoter West (whose success had ruined the Eastern farmers) have been suffering from a disaster not entirely of their own making, we may be better able to judge of their present unrest. They are in a measure responsible for the wild expansion of the early eighties, but they are to be judged leniently for their ignorance of those waves of damage which came from abroad.

Feeling the coils of some mysterious power about them, the farmers, in all honesty, have attributed their misfortunes to the "constriction" in prices, caused, as they think, not by an increased production of wheat throughout the world, but by the "scarcity of gold." This seems hardly an adequate explanation, just at the time when the gold product is doubling itself. If scarcity of gold has been pushing prices down, why does not an abundance of gold push prices up? This explanation of low prices as caused by insufficient gold is so far-fetched that its general use seems inexplicable. The existence of such a theory in explanation of the low price of wheat is so unnatural that it leads one to suspect the presence of a guiding power. Therein is to be found one of the most interesting parts of the present situation. The undereducated man, capable of holding but one idea at a time, and holding that idea fanatically, crushed by the coils of an industrial readjustment, with a system depressed by a speculative debauch, finds supposed helpers in the wiliest managers who have ever entered American politics. This is, in a nutshell, the true philosophy of the movement in favor of free coinage of silver.

Given a large community with innate prejudices against the East, intensified by the dislike born of the relation of debtor to creditor, prostrated by the collapse of the greatest agricultural speculation of modern times, suffering from foreign competition in the world-markets, the opportunity of the tempter is nearly perfect. And the skill of the tempter is satanic. I doubt if ever in our political history we have had more adroit manipulation and strategy than have been displayed by the managers of the silver party. In Congress they have been more than a match in plans and ingenuity for the leaders of the two great parties. Supplied with abundant means by the silver-mining interests, they have "Buncoed" one party or coquetted with another, as suited their interests. While extending their propaganda for years in the ranks of the Democratic party throughout the West and

South, they have bargained with the leaders of the Republican party in Congress for legislation favorable to silver in return for votes for special and private interests. It was in this way that the so-called Sherman Act of 1890 was passed. When they were given an inch they took an ell, until the country stood aghast at finding these silver managers holding the national legislature by the throat, and demanding silver legislation or a stoppage of all old "deals." It was a political brigandage that put the little by-play of Greek bandits to shame. A game of burglary like this in the Capitol at Washington is as audacious as is the seizure of money-tills at high noon on a crowded street.

This, however, was but one part of the great silver conspiracy, the equal of which has never been recorded, and which is too considerable for me to do more than refer to it here. It embraced in its plans years of systematic agitation of the silver doctrines, both by speaking and by writing, among those dissatisfied classes which I have described. The situation of farmers in the West, depressed after a collapse of a speculation in wheat-lands, and of cotton-growers in the South, the price of whose product also had been disturbed by world-causes, was a rich soil for the silver propaganda. It was begun stealthily and secretly, and carried on later with noise and open activity. Newspapers were hired to exploit and advertise silver literature in a way to enlarge their list of subscribers. A literary bureau controlled a systematic distribution of "catchy" and "taking" illustrated reading-matter. The prejudices and antagonisms of classes were appealed to most skillfully. The wheat-farmer and the cotton-grower were for years practically permitted to hear nothing else but the wrongs of silver, the evil effects of gold, and the grinding oppression of the money-lender. As a piece of successful political intrigue and agitation, this propaganda was probably the most effective since the repeal of the Corn Laws. One can have nothing but admiration for the consummate political skill displayed by the managers of the silver party.

How adroitly a situation of agricultural depression, due to an industrial revolution, has been made to serve the dealers in silver, the present presidential campaign gives convincing evidence. At this time, silver is jangling in the ears of those who, a few years hence, will permit only the music of a new craze to be heard. If the conditions which allow of delusions among the farmers were of passing duration, if in a few years we might see Western farming recover from its depression as easily as we see manufacturing and trade readjust themselves after a commercial crisis, the remedy would not be far to seek. But the opening up of new wheat areas to European markets is not a thing that, rising like a wave, like a wave disappears; it is a permanent uplift of the sea-level. It has come to stay, and probably to rise still higher. Farming will go on, and go on profitably; but it will never realize all the bright dreams of the ballooning years in the early eighties. How natural that the seeds of dissatisfaction should grow up in the various forms of protest against existing legislative and social arrangements! It is precisely the expansive, optimistic, speculating American-born in whose minds these erratic developments have taken deepest root. Our less mercurial Germans and shrewder Scandinavians are safer than our Americans, in this day of crazes.

Editorial: THE CHICAGO NOMINEE

THE body of repudiators that has been holding a convention at Chicago during the past week and calling itself the Democratic party, has nominated William J. Bryan of Nebraska for President. The result is somewhat surprising, since Mr. Bryan is a new and untried man, only thirty-six years of age. Only a small fraction of the people of the United States have ever heard of him. All of our Presidents heretofore have been men of experience, sufficiently tested in public life to enable people to form some idea of their capacity and moral fibre. This is not the case with Mr. Bryan. Yet his nomination was not accidental. It was due to the speech which he made on Thursday and to his previous record as a Populist-Democrat in Nebraska. He was found to be precisely of the stamp of Tillman and Altgeld, and of a more attractive personality than either of them. Of all the men voted for in the convention he comes nearest to satisfying the Populists. So say Senator Peffer and ex-Gov. Lewelling of Kansas. It is safe to assume that the Populist convention at St. Louis on the 22d inst. will endorse Bryan, although they might not have endorsed Bland, or Boies, or Blackburn. He will be somewhat less satisfactory to the silver Republicans of the mining states, because they have no

"The Chicago Nominee," *Nation*, LXIII (July 16, 1896), 42.

intention of joining the greenbackers, yet they will probably cast their votes for him.

Mr. Bryan was not a delegate to the convention. He came there leading a contesting delegation. The regular delegates were unseated by the silverite majority and their places were given to Bryan and his crowd. The cheers that greeted him were the measure of his wind power, which is immense. The measure of his specific gravity is to be found in his political career at home. He was carried into Congress on the Democratic tidal wave of 1890, was reelected in 1892, and took a position on the silver question so extreme that he split the Democratic party in his State and lost his seat in Congress. In 1895 the two wings of the party in Nebraska ran separate tickets for Judge of the Supreme Court, and the anti-silver faction polled 8,000 more votes than the Bryan faction. The regular organization of the party remained in their hands, and it was this organization that was cast out by the silverite majority at Chicago in favor of the bolters. His speech to the convention was an appeal to one of the worst instincts of the human heart — that of getting possession of other people's property without the owners' consent. That is what is meant by free coinage at 16 to 1. All business and all obligations rest to-day, have rested for nearly a quarter of a century, on the gold dollar as the unit of value. It is proposed now to substitute a silver dollar for it worth about half as much, and to make this depreciated coin applicable to all existing bargains and contracts. This is not all. It has been alleged over and over again that the programme of the silver propagandists was much more extensive than free silver; that it looked forward to free greenbacks, which are far more attractive to the repudiating tribe. Mr. Bryan gave warning of what is to follow when he said: "The

right to coin money and *issue* money is a function of the Government. It is a part of sovereignty, and can no more be delegated with safety to individuals than we could afford to delegate to private individuals the power to make penal statutes or to levy taxes." If the business community supposed that there were any real danger of this dishonest policy being put into practical operation, there would be a panic and crash the like of which has never been seen in this or any other country. The fact that business remains in a state of quiescence is the best evidence that the proceedings of the roaring mob at Chicago are not taken seriously by the American people.

The nomination of Bryan for President of the United States and the adoption of a platform of repudiation make a pitiful climax for the Democratic party — the party of Jackson, Benton, Seymour, Tilden, Cleveland — the party whose boast has been that it always stood for sound money and never put a depreciated dollar into the hand of labor. The decadence of the party in the past few years, since the Tillmans, Altgelds, Bryans, and Blackburns came to the front and took the leadership, has been melancholy in the extreme. There are signs in plenty that nearly all the men who give character to the party to-day, successors of the great men whose names honor their country's history, will repudiate this ticket and this platform as they would the pest. From all parts of the East and from many in the West and South we hear, not protest merely, but the indignant declaration of Democratic leaders and business men that they will vote the Republican ticket. They consider their honor and their means of livelihood alike involved in this battle. They find something of higher and more immediate concern to their families and to the State than party ties or tariff schedules. They will vote not so much for McKinley and Hobart as against Bryan and repudiation, but their votes will count and their influence will tell from hour to hour and from day to day till the election.

Whether the dissenting Democrats will or ought to nominate a ticket of their own is a question for themselves to decide. Of course the main thing is to beat the ticket of the Repudiators. Everything else is insignificant in comparison, yet opinions may differ as to the best way of accomplishing this result. Our opinion is that the sound-money Democrats, by which term we mean those of intelligence and substance in all parts of the country (in South Carolina and Texas as well as in New York and Massachusetts), will vote for McKinley and Hobart whether there is a sound-money Democratic ticket in the field or not. But the question is not free from difficulty.

Matthew Josephson: THE BRYAN CAMPAIGN

Free Silver is the cow-bird of the reform movement.

HENRY D. LLOYD

NEWS of the sweeping "gold victory" at the St. Louis convention at once electrified and united all the diverse, scattered factions throughout the country which had been taking the popular side in recent controversies; those who had differed in their preferred reforms, those who had favored the popular silver idea in varying degree, now found it possible to combine quickly upon the one issue. The Republican decision was Democracy's opportunity, as the *World* said, June 20, 1896. Would they be bold enough?

Altgeld, who had never been a fanatic of monetary inflation, had spoken out as one of the first leaders to commit the regular Western Democratic Organizations to the cause of "the toiling and producing masses." In Nebraska the Free Silver forces won complete control of their State convention and, in a turbulent outburst, voted down a resolution approving Cleveland's Administration. The Populist leaders, Senator Allen of Nebraska, Weaver, and Taubeneck (chairman of the party), simultaneously aligned themselves beside the regular Western Democrats upon this one issue. "The honest yeomanry of the land," Taubeneck said, were ranged squarely "against the pampered owners of wealth." On behalf of Southern sentiment, now nearly unanimous for bimetallism, Senator Richard (Silver Dick) Bland, of Missouri, who had led the silver movement in the House and the Senate during twenty years, accepted the Republican challenge, declaring in an interview:

The coming fight . . . is to be between the productive masses of the United States, and what might be called the fund-owning classes. The toilers of the East are just as deeply concerned as the toilers of the West and South.

From *The Politicos 1865–1896*, copyright 1938, by Matthew Josephson. Reprinted by permission of Harcourt, Brace and Company, Inc.

On the other hand, the Gold Democrats, led in close formation by Whitney and bearing their compromise resolution on international bimetallism, which was intended actually, as Bryan's Omaha *World-Herald* said, "to stem the tide of genuine bimetallism," offered their concerted opposition. But against the danger from Whitney's men there arose the welcome, the rare, almost unprecedented example of the Silver Republican bolters, who under the lead of the old Stalwart Senator Teller of Colorado threw party loyalty to the winds and marched toward Chicago as volunteers for the silver movement.

Even before the date set for the Republican convention at Chicago, the Populist leaders had known positively that Mr. Teller and his Silverite friends would bolt. Taubeneck wrote confidentially to Ignatius Donnelly from St. Louis:

The Democrats had a large and influential lobby here, moving heaven and earth to get the bolting Republicans to join the Democratic party and go to the Chicago Convention. Bryan was here the entire week. Bland also had a strong lobby on the ground.

In New York, Mr. Pulitzer's *World* during the ensuing summer's fighting veered unaccountably, and threw its powerful voice to the side of Sound Money, charging a conspiracy of Silver Kings to control the Government and double the value of their metal. It was above all "a conspiracy against American labor," by a Silver Trust holding $616,000,000 of mining property. Mr. Teller, the conservative press quickly pointed out, owned some $2,000,000 in silver, lead, and copper-mining securities; the Bonanza Kings of the Pacific slope, John Mackay and Fair, and the gilded California youth William Hearst, heir of the gold-mining Senator,

each possessed fortunes in mining properties reckoned at from $20,000,000 to $40,000,000. Then Senators Jones and Stewart of Nevada were likewise rich mine operators, while the Montana Copper Barons, William A. Clark, J. Augustus Heinze, and Marcus Daly, were also not to be counted among the unwashed poor.

The fears and calculations of the *World* were vastly exaggerated, young Mr. Hearst's newspapers promptly answered. But the intrusion of the great mining interests certainly added to the complexity of the class-sectional movement for Free Silver in 1896. Nearly two years before, the picturesque Marcus Daly, owner of the fabulous Anaconda mines, had entered the fight for the "people's money" in earnest. Through the American Bimetallic League, which employed Bryan as a lecturer and which Daly largely subsidized, powerful, constant, though secret aid was given to the "embattled farmers" who struggled against Eastern "despotism" and "British tyranny." After his death, Daly's books revealed that he and his associates, Heinze and the Hearst Estate, expended no less than $289,000 in securing delegates pledged to Free Silver for the Democratic convention in 1896. During the campaign he gave $50,000 more in one check, according to the statement of Senator J. K. Jones, the Democratic national chairman. Thus the mining operators seem to have acted as an irresponsible, or insurgent, capitalist group at odds, momentarily, with the dominant financial order; they seemed bent on adventures of their own which might lead to an overnight inflation of all commodity and metal values — in which their economic stake was indeed a huge one. The Western mining interests (which obviously hoped to unload their greatly enhanced mining shares upon the New York stock market) added their own special influence and gave an increased "sectional" twist to the class upheaval of 1896. The political champions of the Jacksonian farmers acquired a group of moneyed supporters in the Mining Barons in addition to the mass enthusiasm they already possessed.

The form that the conflict now takes is the traditional one in which the two great divergent interests of society, the classes attached to two different material conditions of existence, two different forms of property, have often fought for supremacy; that of the country against the town, landed property against capital. In the revolution of the Civil War, Northern capital allied with free farmers had fought the domination of the landed economy — more for its own liberation than for the liberation of slaves. Thenceforth out of this Second American revolution, from the emancipated factories of the capitalists and the colossal war debt owed their masters had come new, grievous burdens and inequalities, which the farmers and smallholders now stared at in the 1890's, once more as through a torn veil. The "embattled farmers," West and South, now entered into the fight against new inequalities which were expressed to them in the disparity between the unchanging level of their debts and fixed costs and the falling prices of their goods. They fought, as they declared, for the "cause of humanity" once more, but in reality they fought also for higher wheat, corn, and cotton prices. Here were the limits of their insurgence, and here the points of similarity in interest with the mysterious handful of bimetallist paymasters, who fought for humanity while they intrigued for higher silver, copper, and lead.

The egalitarian doctrines so strongly nourished on the frontier now broke rudely upon our formal, feigning party

contests with unheard-of-force. Yet, behind the characteristic ideas, habits of thought, and *Weltanschauungen* which F. J. Turner attributed to the frontier, we must mark also the economic circumstances which conditioned them. The trade movement of the country moved then (as still, now in great degree) upon the East-West axis; the inner continental region of the West and South as well functioned still under the economy of a colonial relationship with the industrially advanced Northeastern seaboard and Great Lakes region. (Comparable, it has been remarked, to the relations between the backward raw-materials colonies of Africa and the Orient and imperial Britain.) The "free" settlers of the frontier, the "bold peasantry" among whom Peffer, Weaver, Mary Lease, and Bryan were reared, were small independent landholders for the most part, cultivating as much land as their unaided strength could manage, and still resisting the completed, implacable wage system of the older Northeastern communities, the rulers of which moreover "exported" capital to the West, "seized" resources there, sold machinery and railroad, banking, or entrepreneurial services at their own terms. In these social and economic differences between the sections lay the root of the difference in ideology which Turner has described, but before which his analysis stops. The militant ideology of the frontier now gave its own "sectional" tone to the class struggles of the 1890's, to the Tidal Wave in which independent settlers, small proprietors and shopkeepers, organized laborers, and silver-mine or copper-mine owners together moved toward the Democratic Party.

The conflict of profoundly material interests gave, then, a "revolutionary" character to the war of ballots in 1896 — especially as compared with preceding party combats over nuances in taxation, bureaucratic reform, or "personalities." Hence Henry George, writing from the Western battle front, asserted:

The Democratic Party . . . is not the Old Democracy that has existed so long. It is really a new party. . . . Win or lose, the old party lines have been broken.

Yet we must not deceive ourselves as to the true character of the "revolution of the land" in the 1890's. As in the case of the capitalist revolution against "the South" in 1861, so now again we must penetrate behind the ideology and the verbiage of the political orators to the real interests at stake, noting well the limits marked for this uprising. As Marx warns us in his political reflections in the struggles of history we must distinguish between "the super-structure of sentiments, illusions, habits of thought, generalities," and the facts of property interests and material conditions upon which this superstructure is built.

The British landed aristocracy too, as Marx reminds us, when faced with the Industrial Revolution, had insisted that they were fighting for eternal principles of truth, for ancient, constitutional rights and liberties — rather than land rent. While the liberal John Bright, leader of the Manchester industrialists, in turn demanded increased rights and liberties for the lower classes when, in fact, as the Tory philosopher Bagehot points out, he sought "properly enough" increased rights for his own class.

So in America in 1896 the spokesmen of the "Jacksonian farmers," feeling their people to have become exploited "colonists" of the interior, under the yoke of Eastern and foreign financiers, believed, as Bryan told them, that they were en-

gaged in "a fight for the common people." In reality they were fighting for the power and "might" of the corn and wheat lands of the Mississippi Valley and the frontier. But some of their professional brethren, in the Democratic Party and even the Populist Party, while proclaiming the "new battle for freedom" on behalf of the producing masses, were knowingly fighting for the Anaconda mines, for the wealth of the Comstock Lode, for Bonanza Kings, for Daly, Clark, Heinze, Hearst, and others.

Many streams, swollen to torrential size and all flowing together at last, contributed to make the "great silver flood" in which Mr. Whitney and his hopeful little band of Gold Democrats found themselves engulfed promptly upon their arrival in Chicago. The old Tilden-Cleveland hierarchy of the party managers had been completely outmaneuvered. Powerful interests were now at work to carry the masses of the Populist Party as well, with its estimated 2,000,000 voters, into fusion with the silver movement — over the protests of intelligent radicals, such as Lloyd, who mistrusted the "temporary monetary issue."

Under the tumultuous surface excitements, celebrations, parades, and *feux d'artifices* of the eve of the Chicago convention, the organized battalions of professionals carried on their planned and paid work, furnishing brass bands, pennants, or "spontaneous" bloodcurdling demonstrations, as the occasion required. Even the most naive of the silver ideologues who spoke there commented with surprise on the perfect unison and discipline with which the audience responded "like a trained choir" to his arguments. This effect Bryan attributed, as he hints, to his own eloquence rather than to a large claque, carefully organized by the Bimetallic League and following a premeditated plan. Yet it is true also that natural and life forces may burst over the banks laid for them; history too sometimes surprises, and exceeds the schemes, the frames, set by wirepullers and their claquers at party conventions.

II

The "logic of events," the tactics for the electoral campaign, as envisaged since the autumn of 1895, had pointed to an unqualified demand for Free Silver and the breaking of the political alliance made between the capitalistic Eastern Republicans and the Western farmers in 1860. The silver movement after capturing the Democratic Party must take over a portion of the Republican Party as well. This was what Altgeld meant in the spring of 1895 when he remarked that half of the Republicans in his own State of Illinois were Free Silver men, and predicted that by taking a clear stand for silver the Democrats would win their greatest victory. This step, moreover, was made unavoidable after the adoption of an outright "gold plank" in June by Mr. Hanna's convention at St. Louis.

Many witnesses testify that from the opening of the Democratic convention (from which Bland, as a candidate, was absent) Altgeld became its dominating spirit, its "brain and will." He headed the Illinois delegation, which was pledged to the Free Silver cause. In intelligence he towered above the others easily; none equaled him in firmness, courage, and practical political sagacity. The men of the press came to him more than to anyone else for information on the tide of the battle. Each candidate wooed Altgeld for support of his nomination; Jones of Arkansas, Tillman, Bryan, and the other Silverite leaders present all worked with him for the capture of the necessary two-thirds majority of the convention.

In Free Silver conferences and secret caucuses before the convention opened it was carefully arranged that when the contesting Nebraska delegations came up with their credentials, the Bryan delegation should be seated in place of the Gold Democrat delegation. Then by the unseating of four of the Michigan delegation (through legalistic methods), and by augmentation of the number of delegates from the Territories, a two-thirds majority was to be assured. Altgeld was the prime mover in these preliminary maneuvers. Cajoled, threatened, or challenged by leaders of the different factions, the man whom President Cleveland had insulted, and the whole Eastern press had tried to crush with calumny, led the Democratic Party relentlessly to the adoption of the "new heresies" of silver money.

Teller, the Republican bolter, was seriously considered by Altgeld for the presidential nomination as a means of breaking old party lines. Naming the former Republican would have set "principle" above party, as in 1860; but he would not have been a popular choice among the rank-and-file politicians. Hence Bland was the predominant choice of the Western men. Yet it was a handicap that he was a "southerner," represented Missouri, and that his wife was a Catholic. Senators Jones and Vest were old men. Governor Boies of Iowa was one of the stronger of several Favorite Sons, but he also came under the onus of having been a Republican up to recently. Among lesser Favorite Sons was Bryan, too young at thirty-six, with only Nebraska and several Indian Territory delegates as his following, though the politicians as well as the silvermine owners behind the scenes felt well disposed toward him because of his speaking power and his faithful services to the American Bimetallic League. There is reason to believe that Altgeld at first favored him for the Vice-Presidency as a running mate to Bland.

In the contest for the post of temporary chairman to preside over the convention, Bryan, eager for this office, was passed over as a matter of seniority. He was rewarded, however, by being named to speak in the debate over the platform; then by a last-minute shift of the program, he was selected for the strategic last place, closing the whole debate on the silver resolution. All these positions were carried over the desperate opposition of Whitney and David Hill. As the convention opened preliminary arrangements were carried out as expected, with the vital steering committees and subcommittees in the hands of the "radicals." Whitney and his friends were in despair. They could make at best only a demonstration to "save the esprit de corps," that is, hold together the party's Eastern wing for future emergency action. At the convention the once invincible Whitney seemed to abandon the fight completely.

William Bryan of Nebraska, the poor country-town lawyer, had for eight years been carving out a career in politics after an old American pattern. The mind of this born elocutionist, in the view of William Allen White, who knew him, may well have been stuffed with the spirit of old steel engravings such as covered the walls of his library in Lincoln, Nebraska — engravings of Jefferson, Jackson, Lincoln, Webster, and above all, of Henry Clay, "towering almost ten feet high in foreground, badly out of perspective, pleading with the lilliputian senators — all in stocks and tail coats . . . all dignified and serious, wrapped in improving meditation. . . . Bryan all his life seemed to draw from this picture his fine Fourth Reader views . . . of life." It may have been true likewise, as others felt, that Bryan was: "Not really able nor even

clear headed, lacking capacity as a thinker"; that his abstinence from drink and tobacco, his religious piety and ill-concealed evangelism, made him a little "the humbug" to hardened professional colleagues, upon whom he too must depend in the last resort.

Yet Bryan's very "simplicity" led him to embrace historic opportunities which the wise old men of the East could not, or would rather not, see. In his campaigns, in his lecture tours on behalf of the American Bimetallic League, he saw with his own eyes the force stirring at the "grass roots" of the republic. Then his evangelism, his single-minded fanaticism, like Cromwell's, was suited to the revolutionary times, and lent point and astonishing force to his speech.

On the other hand, by his own convictions Bryan was far from being the "dangerous revolutionary" whom his frightened adversaries pictured. The limits of his protest (like the limitations of his thought) were well defined, and became more evident later as his career extended itself prosaically, after the glamour, the excitation, the intoxicated rhetoric of his great hours in 1896 had passed. He mourned at the bier of the pure-hearted Lyman Trumbull, but differed strongly with the old war Republican's later socialistic views. He flirted successfully with the Populists in Nebraska and won their co-operation in his creditable, though unsuccessful, fight for the United States Senatorship in 1894. Ignatius Donnelly of Minnesota said of him: "We put him to school, and he wound up by stealing the schoolbooks." He worked with the Populists, they believed him one of them; yet he was not of them.

The Populists, the radical wing of the farmers of the Middle Border, were bent on reversing the old Jacksonian and liber-

tarian doctrines, which had sought free
land, freedom from governmental or
authoritarian restrictions, and now sought
rather increased national government
support to guarantee their old liberties.
They clamored for a "paternalistic" Federal ownership of monopolies in railroads
and grain elevators, for the extension of
government Treasury facilities in farm
credits and warehousing. Monetary inflation was but incidental, a means to an end
of sweeping and rational reform. Here
Bryan did not follow where they led. On
these radical demands he was vague or
silent.

It was the singular role of this "evangelist and crusader, with a great musical,
vibrant voice, fashioned for political purposes," to check the impetus of the Farmers' Alliance (Populist) movement, divert
its logical drive for genuine land reform,
and shift the objective of the land uprising
to the monetary issue solely. Glossing
over the laborious reforms demanded by
the agrarian radicals, this young Christian
Statesman led his followers to the social
impasse of monetary inflation, from which
he promised them untold benefit — above
all, a longed-for redistribution of wealth
— would certainly flow.

Bryan, finally, saw no harm in carrying
on an opportunistic collaboration with
the Silver and Copper Barons, feeling
sincerely that attainment of their objec-
tives would aid his own people too. Such
a compromise was perfectly typical of the
Puritan temperament. The aggressive
mining interests that worked behind the
scenes, according to some observers, seriously considered Bryan as the most likely
figure for the plan of a "stampede," whose
outcome none as yet could foretell. For
Bryan, though less known than the older
politicians, attracted the Populists, and
might provide the best bridge leading

to fusion with their important voting
strength. "Bryan is a Populist in all but
the name," one of the agrarian leaders
wrote to Weaver, in the early spring of
1896. He proposed that Bryan should
head the Populist and Democratic tickets
both.

While without modesty about his ambitions, there was something meek and
patient as well as practical in the way in
which Bryan advanced his cause. His
humility avoided enmities. Numerous
politicians and delegates recalled afterward that Bryan spoke to them seriously
in asking their support at the 1896 convention; although, as Champ Clark afterward said, he seemed to be the only one
who believed in his chances. But hope-
fully he persisted, like other Favorite
Sons, in reaching as many people as he
could, holding himself the most available
"regular" Democrat from a "doubtful"
Northern State, and destined to be chosen
by elimination. Bryan and his wife wrote
thousands of letters to leaders and members of State Organizations concerning
platform resolutions, pledges, and the
support of his own incredible candidacy.
"I perhaps was personally acquainted
with more delegates than any other man
who was mentioned as a candidate,"
Bryan observed.

Carefully the young man wheeled himself into position to be struck by presidential lightning. He was delighted when
he contrived to appear in the momentous
debate over the silver plank, serving as
one of the "keynoters" of the Western
silver uprising within the party. It was a
further stroke of luck that he was the last
speaker for the silver faction, and was
given additional time in return for aug-
mented speaking time asked by the opposing Gold Democrats — Hill, Vilas, and
Russell. Bryan's speech was long pre-

pared, woven from old strands of ideas and phrases used in lectures throughout the South and the Mississippi Valley.

As he waited for his hour, a friend, Clark Howell, editor of the Atlanta *Constitution,* sent him a note scribbled on an envelope: "This is a great opportunity." Bryan, according to his own recollections, wrote in reply: "You will not be disappointed," and sent the envelope back.

III

Though the external behavior of the "revolutionary mob" which overran the Chicago convention may have been enough to frighten the Eastern Democrats, inwardly the convention's action reflected order and a firm command. Altgeld, its directing spirit, though a semi-invalid, sat quietly in his place among the delegates, always holding himself impassive, as under an iron control.

On Tuesday, July 7, the recommendation of the party's national committee — which traditionally was followed — that Senator David B. Hill act as "temporary chairman," that is, preside over the proceedings of the nominating convention, was voted down uproariously by a majority of 556 to 349, John W. Daniel, of Virginia, an ardent bimetallist, receiving the office. It was the opening blow and a finishing stroke: "the sceptre of political power passed from the strong, certain hands of the East to the feverish, headstrong mob of the West and South." The too crafty Hill was like a man who was out of his element.

On the following day the credentials of the Nebraska prosilver delegates, Bryan at their head, were passed upon, and with the Territorial delegates a two-thirds majority was achieved for Free Silver, and the obstructive power of the minority eliminated.

While the convention, waiting for further business, gave itself over to celebrating the overthrow of the Goldbugs, Altgeld was called by tremendous, sustained ovations to make an impromptu speech. In a brief, vigorous statement, he set the keynote: "no compromise" in the party resolutions. "With his sharply chiselled French Revolution face, his high, ringing voice, his bitter vehemence of manner, and his facility for epithet," as a hostile journalist described him, Altgeld figured largely in the horrific myth of a bogey-man which gripped all the conservative classes. He was pictured as

the most dangerous influence in the convention having the stamp of the agitator who, when the bludgeon had failed of its full work, would be ready with the poisoned knife, and who, in leading a victory-drunken mob, would not hesitate to follow pillage with the torch.

Yet the vast majority of the audience applauded to the echo their hero who might have had the nomination if he had been eligible. It was the music of consoling vindication for Altgeld.

Thursday, July 9, which began with the reading of the platform by Senator J. K. Jones on behalf of the Resolutions Committee, saw the climax of the convention. By its platform the new Democratic Party which was being born took the unprecedented step of disavowing the ruling national Administration of its own President. Mr. Cleveland was denounced in so many plain words for making private contracts for bond sales to the Morgan banking syndicate and increasing the national debt in time of peace; he was condemned for his highhanded use of the court injunction and Federal troops; more, the august "House of Lords," our

Supreme Court, for its recent decisions was also visited with the party's disapproval. Then the silver plank was read before listeners, tense, bitter or jubilant:

We are unalterably opposed to monometallism, which has locked fast the prosperity of an industrial people in the paralysis of hard times. . . . We demand the free and unlimited coinage of both silver and gold at the present legal ratio of 16 to 1, without waiting for the aid or consent of any other nation.

There was to be no compromise. Pitchfork Ben Tillman, as arranged, began the debate upon the platform resolutions with a fierce castigation of the President, in a style which recalled plainly the secessionist days of 1860. The men of the South, he cried, were up in arms against their exploiters:

We of the South have burned our bridges behind us so far as the Eastern Democrats are concerned. . . . We denounce the Administration of President Cleveland as undemocratic and tyrannical. . . . A plutocratic despotism is sought to be established.

In answer, Hill of New York rose to the defense of his old rival, Cleveland, and spoke also for the minority opposing Free Silver coinage. With his usual smacking emphasis upon the word "Democrat" he began:

I am a Democrat, but I am not a revolutionist. My mission here to-day it to unite, not to divide — to build up, not to destroy. . . . My friends, I speak more in sorrow than in anger. You know what this platform means to the East. . . . We want the principles of Jefferson and Jackson. We want no greenback currency. . . . We want no paper currency.

Hill, the most conciliatory speaker for the Gold Democracy, was little heard by the tempestuous men of the Chicago convention. Even less Senator Vilas, of Wisconsin, Cleveland's former Postmaster General, though he gave warning of a bloody debacle to come: "Perhaps somewhere in this country there lurks a Robespierre, a Danton, a Marat?" Nor did the delegates and the spectators, by turns turbulent, hostile, or bored, give heed to the sickly Governor Russell of Massachusetts, who, after pleading in a weak voice against repudiation, exclaimed finally that "our country, if not this convention, will listen to our protest."

Bryan of Nebraska now strode toward the platform "two steps at a time." He had the bearing of "a strong-limbed, strong-lunged" athlete as he stood for an instant facing "the wild crowd. . . . It had been known for hours that the convention might be stampeded for the Nebraskan. . . . Earsplitting noises were heard; waves of scarlet fans danced in the galleries." The whole convention, the moment, demanded impatiently a voice to express its purpose, its hope. Bryan had himself marvelously well in hand, as he relates, having been thoroughly prepared since the night before; in his mind was the epopee of the "cross of gold" which he had been saving for such an occasion, "recognizing its fitness for the conclusion of a climax." Many of those who were present also attest to the "miracle" of the young speaker's mastery over the crowd, as we remember the enchantment of a great actor in our youth. With a gesture he silenced the long roar of applause that had greeted him; the clear, soaring voice began its work.

His opening words were as modest as they were courteous. He was not so "presumptuous" as to measure himself against the more distinguished gentlemen who preceded him; but, he cried:

The humblest citizen in all the land, when clad in the armor of a righteous cause, is stronger than all the hosts of error. I come to speak to you in defense of a cause as holy as the cause of liberty — the cause of humanity.

He passed over the bitter personal issues raised by the reigning President. "The individual is but an atom; he is born, he acts, he dies; but principles are eternal; and this has been a contest over a principle." Thus Bryan, "with . . . the zeal which inspired the crusaders who followed Peter the Hermit," clothed the interests of the silver Democrats in the noblest ideology.

In the face of so much legend that the sense of Bryan's appeal was "socialistic," we must note the precise line of his reasoning, even at the emotional crest of his oratory. In its essence it reflects not a landless, toolless proletarian opposition, but the mentality and social relationships of the lower middle class, the numerous body of small-holders, artisans, country lawyers, and shopkeepers at crossroads to whom Bryan belonged and whom he would lead in a crusade against the *big* property-holders and *big* capitalists. Thus with a significant and deeply characteristic stroke of dialectics — paradoxical and fallacious at once — he defined the businessman anew in a passage which he was proud of and inserted at the last moment as the only new material among his old silver arguments. The Eastern Democrats had accused the silver men of "disturbing business," and Bryan, turning to the gold delegates, said:

. . . we reply that you have disturbed our business by your course. We say to you that you have made the definition of a business man too limited in its application. The man who is employed for wages is as much a business man as his employer, the attorney in a country town is as much a business man as the corporation counsel in a great metropolis; the merchant at the cross-roads store is as much a business man as the merchant of New York; the farmer who goes forth in the morning and toils all day — who begins in the spring and toils all summer — and who by the application of brain and muscle to the natural resources of the country creates wealth, is as much a business man as the man who goes upon the board of trade and bets upon the price of grain; the miners who go down a thousand feet into the earth . . . and bring forth from their hiding places the precious metals to be poured into the channels of trade are as much business men as the few financial magnates who, in a back room, corner the money of the world. We come to speak for this broader class of business men.

With a reasoning familiar to our own age also, Bryan drew a line of cleavage between the small or petit-bourgeois capitalist and the great finance capitalist of the world money centers. In such argument, as in such a "revolution," there is confusion and contradiction, just as there is latent discord, jealousy, and sectional hostility among the conglomeration which forms the party of the middle class, the landed interests and producing interests, fused by an hour of crisis and opportunity. Thus, unlike Bebel in Germany and Jaures in France, rational economic doctrinaires who were at this time directing the Social Democratic movement of the working class in Europe, Bryan addressed himself to numerous divisions and groups in the body politic, offering something to teach. For the producing and toiling masses he seems to attack the ruling financial class, and proposes a redistribution of wealth, saying:

There are those who believe that, if you will only legislate to make the well-to-do prosperous, their prosperity will leak through on those below. The Democratic idea, however, has been that if you legislate to make the masses prosperous, their prosperity will find its way up through every class which rests upon them.

But repeatedly he turns to his dominant theme, the defense and exaltation of the landed interest; he apotheosizes the frontiersman, the pioneer. Once more Jefferson's "chosen" people and Jackson's "embattled farmers" are fighting for cheaper money and relief from their debts. He extols

the hardy pioneers who have braved all the dangers of the wilderness, who have made the desert to blossom as the rose — the pioneers away out there (pointing to the West), who rear their children near to Nature's heart, where they can mingle their voices with the voices of the birds — out there where they have erected schoolhouses for the education of their young, churches where they praise their Creator, and cemeteries where rest the ashes of their dead — these people, we say, are as deserving of the consideration of our party as any people in the country. It is for these that we speak. . . . Our war is not a war of conquest; we are fighting in the defense of our homes, our families, and prosperity.

It is significant how he passes over in the most general terms concrete issues of tariff, of statism, of the regulation of monopolies, raised by the truly radical farm leaders, while harping on the theme of cheap money.

Did the great cities favor the gold standard? But the great cities themselves

rest upon our broad and fertile prairies. Burn down your cities and leave our farms, and your cities will spring up again as if by magic;

but destroy our farms and the grass will grow in the streets of every city in the country.

As the measured words of the orator rolled over the great hall the tense crowd responded rhythmically with crashes of applause to the points brought home. At one climax, Bryan's voice rose, and he gesticulated in graceful pattern:

We have petitioned, and our petitions have been scorned; we have entreated, and our entreaties have been disregarded; we have begged, and they have mocked when our calamity came. We beg no longer; we entreat no more; we petition no more. (A dramatic pause.) *We defy them.*

The last words, "We defy them!" were flung out with a most impressive movement of the speaker's whole body; they rang with an accent of "superb disdain," and were followed by an outburst of mad cheering from 20,000 throats. Then amid renewed silence, in more subdued but intense accents, Bryan launched into the famous conclusion of his speech, whose meaning has been much overlooked, closing with an appeal to patriotism in the face of the traditional enemy, England. The mixed sectional-class conflict was given a memorable nationalistic or jingo hue. Must we wait for England to decree bimetallism in the world before we moved, he asked? It was the "issue of 1776" again.

If they dare to come out in the open . . . we will fight them to the uttermost. Having behind us the producing masses of this nation and the world, supported by the commercial interests, the laboring interests, and the toilers everywhere, we will answer their demand for a gold standard by saying to them: *You shall not press down upon the brow of labor this crown of thorns, you shall not crucify mankind upon a cross of gold.*

The hall awoke from its hypnotic silence in a bedlam of cheering and parading which lasted for half an hour. The Goldbugs were undone. The Western Democracy had found its leader. The various State delegations forming in processions gathered before the Nebraska section and dipped their flags before the Nebraska standard. Only the Eastern gold men sat sullen before this largely spontaneous uproar, and in the vote upon the platform which followed cast their minority ballots in a dying opposition. According to the conservative press of New York and Chicago, it was a "political debauch," an "orgy," likened to the opening of the Reign of Terror in Paris. "Hell has broken loose in Chicago," Wickham Stead cabled to London.

Other more discriminating observers noted the unusual enthusiasm and spontaneity which marked this convention, an unfamiliar phenomenon at our popular political gatherings, and utterly absent at the preceding Republican convention at St. Louis. One wrote, in London:

It was essentially the most genuine and impromptu political movement that has been known for many a decade. It was really the birth of a new party — a party devoted in spirit, what ever its mistakes of method, to human rights and human progress, to the welfare of the common people, to the promulgation of a newer and truer Democracy.

Bryan of Nebraska — his words had been flashed throughout the country by telegraph, making a profound or a terrifying impression — had introduced a new spirit into the formal contests of the parties, evoked a national, quasi-revolutionary impulse on behalf of silver-money inflation of a scope which few men, least of all the rather shifty mine operators who originally sponsored silver coinage, could have calculated in advance. The little-

known Western politician, by the "miracle" of his speech, was as a consequence to be catapulted into the presidential nomination and an electoral contest which would shake the very foundation stones of the republic. Bryan might have been nominated by acclamation at the moment his speech ended; but the balloting which was to follow the adoption of the silver platform was held over until next day.

"Bryan, Bryan! No crown of thorns, no cross of gold!" the paraders and revelers sang.

Bryan, whose candidacy had been "amusing" on the morning before July 10, was second only to Bland in the first three ballots and assumed the lead on the fourth. Another adjournment, and a hasty conference was called by the leaders and wirepullers; then on the fifth ballot the "break" came, and a majority was won by the Boy Orator and "tribune of the people." On the following day the press significantly reported:

The Democratic National Convention nominated William J. Bryan of Nebraska for President. . . . Withdrawals . . . brought the gold reserve . . . below $100,000,000.

A man of wealth, Arthur Sewall, a banker, shipbuilder, and railway director who happened to believe in Free Silver, was then named as the vice-presidential candidate.

The hysterical crowds who came to his hotel carried the Nebraskan upon their shoulders and called for a speech. "My friends," he responded, "I feel this is going to be a campaign of sentiment. This is to be a fight for the common good."

IV

News of the unheard-of proceedings at Chicago aroused consternation in high

Republican circles. Not only was the choice of the young Silverite orator from the Northwest drastic in itself, but what was worse, the party's disavowal of its own Democratic Administration as "plutocratic" and "despotic" upset traditions, broke all the established rules of the chivalric tournament of party politics. The insurgent Democratic leadership had exchanged the wooden lances of fictive election debates for the sharpened scythes and pitchforks of class-sectional issues. Where the Republican strategists had counted that they would pass the summer good-humoredly in recounting the errors of the party in office, blaming Hard Times, poor prices, blundering tariff laws, even unfavorable weather, on the incompetence of the opposition, where they had trusted fondly that even a Republican "rag doll" would be carried into office by the rhythmically recurrent negative discharges of the biparty system, they must literally battle for their lives.

So Mr. Hanna felt. The Republicans had committed themselves, to be sure, to the gold dollar. But their campaign tactics, as outlined on the morrow of the St. Louis convention involved mentioning as little as possible this unpleasant item. "I am a Tariff man, standing on a Tariff platform," the Major had said at once to his counselors. "This money matter is unduly prominent. In thirty days you won't hear anything about it." Mark Hanna, who had very properly been chosen chairman of the Republican National Committee, had expressed thorough agreement with this view. But Judge William Day, an active associate who was present at the conference, had remarked: "In my opinion, in thirty days, you won't hear of anything else."

With the young Mr. Bryan fanning general discontent and offering an "immediate cure" for all the nation's ills, they were confronted not with a political campaign but with a "revolution." Hanna, who had planned an agreeable yachting vacation to Nantucket after so much hard work, wrote to McKinley July 16:

The Chicago convention has changed everything. It has knocked out my holiday and cruise along the New England coast. The campaign will be work and hard work. I consider the situation in the West quite alarming as business is all going to pieces and idle men will multiply rapidly. With this communistic spirit abroad the cry of "free silver" will be catching.

In conferences of late July, the Republican managers agreed to forget the tariff question and face the currency issue squarely. This meant a "campaign of education" upon the financial question, hard ungrateful work among broad masses of people who were ill equipped to learn or understand; enormous efforts and enormous sums of money must be expended to this end. Moreover, this year, instead of carrying on work in a half-dozen "doubtful" States, they must fight up and down the whole country.

It was a discouraging prospect. The air was thick with gloom — markets sank, stocks fell, gold began to be drawn freely from the government Treasury. Hanna now resolutely made Organization plans upon a larger scale than he had anticipated. He arranged for two national headquarters instead of one — at Chicago as well as at New York. Then, on July 26, he left Canton and Major McKinley and came to New York on a first, secret mission of the campaign.

The decision taken at the People's Party convention at St. Louis, in mid-July, seemed but to augment the alarming class-sectional character of the struggle this year. To St. Louis also the agents of the silver cabal quickly repaired, bent as they had been for two years on achieving fusion between the Populists and the Democrats. This to Marcus Daly, and to allied Silverite politicians like Senators Stewart, Jones of Nevada, and Pettigrew, as to the veteran People's Party leaders, Weaver, Allen, and Sockless Jerry Simpson, would break the bonds between the rural West and the financial Northeast, and with it the hegemony of the Eastern Goldbugs.

These men now contrived to manage the Populist convention by means of wire-pulling as effective as any party assembly ever saw. Henry Demarest Lloyd in a letter of the time reflected on how curious it was that "the new party, the Reform party, the People's party, should be more boss-ridden, gang-ruled, gang-gangrened than the two old parties of monopoly." But yesterday this well-meaning reformer had joined the Populists with enthusiasm and worked to bring about a coalition between farmers and union labor, convinced that "the people are about to take possession of the property of the people." Today bitter doubts assailed him.

The veteran Populist and Farmers' Alliance organizers were now within sight of victory, power, and office, after so many years of wandering in the wilderness. Did they not have the substance of what they wanted in Bryan? asked Simpson of Kansas. Bryan was a Populist in all but name, and what did the party name matter?

Amid scenes of emotional storm usually attending the farmers' party conventions, while the highly extroverted Mary Elizabeth Lease nearly burst a blood vessel, and the chairman burst his galluses out of sheer excitement, Senator Allen, the "incorruptible" Weaver, and other leaders steered the convention toward fusion, despite a stubborn opposing minority. This consisted in part of clear-sighted prolabor radicals such as Lloyd, in part

of the idealistic Southern Populists who had faced prejudice and violence in their efforts to erect a truly progressive third-party organization, free from Southern Bourbonism and official corruption. (It was becoming really a second "white man's party" in a region devoted to the single-party system.)

"By the time this money question is settled," argued Senator Marion Butler of North Carolina, . . . the great transportation question — that great question which stands side by side with the money question — will be upon you." The problems of transportation, the trusts and monopolies — these were what the People's Party had come into existence to fight, he urged.

Other opponents of fusion felt that the moment was a turning-point in their young party, which had grown in a few years to 1,500,000 votes and dominated a half-dozen Western and Southwestern States. Would it not be the "death knell" of their movement, they asked, if they were swallowed up in the Democracy?

The People's Party, as we have remarked, had risen as a "peasants' party" of the Middle Border and the South, advocating carefully studied land reforms, popular credit institutions and co-operative marketing measures, which at the period represented a realistic view of their problems. Slowly, despite special difficulties, it approached coalition with trade-union groups and even socialists of various colors. Must whatever gains in educational and cohesive force the persistence of their Organization promised be now jeopardized, gambled away by the opportunists who cried with Weaver and Allen *"Win this time"*?

The minority stoutly urged a course defined in an unfortunate phrase: to stick to "the middle of the road," that is, drive between the two big parties. But the answer from Allen carried the day:

Do you want . . . a President who is in favor of . . . Government ownership of railroads and telegraphs?

I do not want my constituents to say to me that the Populists have been advocates of reforms, when they could not be accomplished, but when the first ray of light appeared and the people were looking with expectancy and anxiety for relief, the party was not equal to the occasion; that it was stupid; it was blind; it kept "in the middle of the road" and missed the golden opportunity.

Weaver for his part welcomed the "new Pentecost," and would not refuse the proffered assistance of 3,000,000 Silver Democrats and 1,000,000 Silver Republicans "simply because they have shown the good sense to come with an organized army ready for battle." Bryan was a champion of the people. Let us go to the rescue of this gallant knight, "assailed by the sleuth hounds of the money power of the world," he exhorted.

At the last moment, after having agreed to nominate Bryan of Nebraska by acclamation, the veteran Populists gagged at approving of Sewall, the banker and railroad man, for the Vice-Presidency. The fire-eating Thomas Watson of Georgia was proposed instead. A tense contest was fought over this issue, in the midst of which came a somewhat chivalrous telegram from Bryan, refusing the Populists' nomination if his running mate were not also named by them. But this dispatch was highhandedly withheld from the convention by Senator Allen, and the Populists, in ignorance, proceeded to name Bryan and Watson for their ticket.

In their platform, too, the Populists showed radical deviations from the Democrats, demanding besides free and unlimited coinage of silver the establishment of postal savings banks, direct election of Senators and of Presidents and Vice-Presidents, the initiative and referendum, government ownership of public utilities, and Federal public-works expenditure for the unemployed. In this anomalous manner they responded to the "bugle call" of fusion, amid frenzied demonstrations, singing, and waving of the American flag.

Lloyd, a bitter observer of the last minute proceedings, wrote on July 18, 1896:

. . . The poor people are throwing up their hats in the air for those who promise "to lead them out of the wilderness" by way of the currency route. . . . The people are to be kept wandering forty years in the currency labyrinth, as they have for the last forty years been led up and down the tariff hill.

He reflected further that this "fortuitous collection of the dissatisfied" lacked all grasp of any fundamental principle which might keep a genuine party movement together.

The Free Silver movement is a fake. Free Silver is the cow-bird of the Reform movement. It waited until the nest had been built by the sacrifices and labour of others, and then it laid its eggs in it. . . . The People's party has been betrayed. . . . No party that does not lead its leaders will ever succeed.

The intense division of opinion in the press during the 1896 campaign showed how the nation was split into two great sections. South of Mason and Dixon's line and the Ohio River generally, and west of the Mississippi, Mr. Bryan was a Tribune of the People; he was leader of a "new battle for freedom" to the Duluth *Herald;* and a true knight of the West "fighting for the people," according to the Kansas City *Times.*

But north and east of this boundary, the press and the pulpit thundered in a voice of fury against Bryan and his followers: "Down with the fanatics!" called the

Springfield *Republican;* "National dis-
honor, private robbery, the exaltation of
anarchy . . . the damnation of the Constitution," were the patent objects of the
silver movement to the Philadelphia
Inquirer. In Chicago, now the financial
metropolis of the older Middle West, the
press generally echoed McKinley's partisan denunciation of the Democratic convention as "an aggregation of populism,
socialism and idiocy," precipitating a
crisis "greater than the Civil War." But
in New York's newspapers emotion
strained mere words; the Bryan movement was commonly treated as

the hysterical declaration of a reckless and
lawless crusade of sectional animosity and
class antagonism. . . . No wild-eyed and
rattle-brained horde of the red flag ever proclaimed a fiercer defiance of law, precedent,
order, and government.

The gentle souls who edited the family
journal *Harper's Weekly* held that the
spirits of Danton, Robespierre, and Marat
(in the form of Bryan, Altgeld, and Tillman) had risen again to impose the Revolutionary Terror of 1793. Bryan, moreover, the "baby orator," was "clay to the
hand of the potter" — John Altgeld, who
was portrayed in caricature almost each
week of the campaign as a ruffianly Cata-
line, concealing a torch in his gown (!)
and using the head of Bryan as his mask.

In the East, the New York *Morning
Journal* alone, among important newspapers, spoke for the Democratic side.
Against the advice of his editors, the
young William Hearst, whose father was
Marcus Daly's late partner, threw himself
into the silver movement with all his resources, and regaled a large public with
Homer Davenport's savage cartoons of
Mr. Hanna, and Henry George's bugle
blasts for the new crusade.

Bryan himself emphasized the sectional
nature of the conflict from the beginning
when he alluded, in an unfortunate
phrase, to the East, and to New York particularly, as "the enemy's country," which
he intended to invade.

Professor Frederick J. Turner, at the
time, wrote also of the upheavals of the
day as a sectional conflict. The West, he
said, was a debtor region; the West had
been built up with borrowed capital. But
now, not only was money scarce, but free
or cheap land as well; "profoundly dissatisfied," eagerly agitating the problem
of the monetary unit, "discontent is demanding an extension of governmental
activity in its behalf."

The West still engendered its separate
ideology. Despite an occasional Collis
Huntington, or a Jim Hill, there was relatively less inequality of station and property in the prairies of the Granger States,
the Middle Border, and the plateaus and
slopes of the Rocky Mountains. The fac-
tory, with its "wage slavery," was still a
weaker element in the Western economy;
men clung to an older, simpler American
concept of democracy, and made in the
West a last gallant stand against the triumph of high capitalism.

It was in New York City, where the
inhabitants of monstrous shadowed slums
dwelt within a stone's throw of the Gothic
or Renaissance castles of brownstone
built for financial nabobs, it was here,
where in all their contrasting extremes of
grandeur and misery the "two nations"
were to be seen side by side, that the old
American doctrines of democracy appeared weakest. It was here, in the financial and social center of the country, that
the old Eastern leadership of the Democrats reached the momentous decision to
abandon their party.

Party loyalty and party discipline had
been fed to our political leaders with their

mothers' milk. Yet now Whitney, from his palace on Fifth Avenue, denounced the majority Democrats. After the convention Whitney stated publicly that he would support neither his party's candidate nor its platform. He and the other men of capital who had been patrons of the Democratic Party had discovered that they were "men of principle" first, and Democrats afterward. It was a "fight for the preservation of National Honor," Whitney asserted. What troubled him was the slowness of the Republicans to "grasp at once the seriousness of the situation." He advised that they give up the irrelevant tariff issue and concentrate upon the money question. Else, a Sound Money Democratic Party must be launched at once.

President Cleveland, sitting in the White House alone, feeding upon his bitterness, as he has been described, also underwent a crisis of "class consciousness." This "man of the people" was soon to leave his office considerably richer than when he arrived, twelve years before, thanks to his association with Whitney, Stetson, and Benedict; and he too discovered that it was time to place principle above party and forego all compromise. The Silverites were "madmen," or "criminals" worthy of the penitentiary, he burst out in a private letter to one of his friends at this point. To another he said with feeling: ". . . It will be our duty to stand by our guns and let the party go."

A *formula* was sought by which the Eastern wing of the Democratic Party could, in a body, desert and go over to the enemy. Great financiers, such as Whitney, railroad masters and bankers, who had worked with the party's Inner Circle since the days of Tilden, men such as Belmont, Charles Fairchild, Jim Hill, and the more recent convert Henry Villard, having failed to hold their party, prepared to destroy it from within. The project of a new frank class alignment which was implicit in their plans was most bluntly expressed by the banker Fairchild, who insisted that a third ticket must be put in the field, saying:

We want to see the defeat of the Democratic ticket, and we shall try to draw away as many votes as we can from it. . . . Of course, we shall find no fault with those of our friends who cast a straight vote for McKinley.

The problem was a delicate one; it was intended that any new party should not draw strength from the Republicans. In fact Stillman, of the National City Bank, strongly urged his friends among the Eastern Democrats not to run a separate candidate. Dickinson of Michigan and Senator Vilas of Wisconsin, however, busied themselves with Mr. Whitney's party of Gold Democrats, which in the Border Southern States was to answer the pretended partisan scruples of their followers. A rather stillborn party of Gold Democrats was hastily set up (at a very tame "national convention") and a ticket, consisting of Senator John Palmer of Illinois and General Buckner of Kentucky, was offered to the electorate. This party of bolters, Bryan declared, were "in the employ of trusts and syndicates and combinations," and were "leaving their party for their party's good." Yet they accumulated 135,000 votes in November, and in at least one important State helped to tip the balance of the votes for the Republicans. Moreover, the esprit de corps of the Eastern wing was thus held together, as Whitney had hoped, for revival of the old control in the event of Bryan's defeat.

Many of the Cleveland Democrats, however, wasted no time over the Gold Democrats, but went wholeheartedly over to Mr. Hanna's party. Henry Villard, one of the earliest deserters, launched the National Sound Money League, which numbered William Rockefeller as one of its chief subscribers. James J. Hill brought his political power in six Northwestern States to the Republican Party. To J. Pierpont Morgan he wrote on July 15, 1896:

There is an epidemic craze for free silver among the farmers, and to some extent among those who receive wages or salaries. . . . The McKinley managers should get to work *at once*. . . . I will do anything or everything in my power to further the end we all have in view.

Once more, as in the Jacksonian Era, there were ranged on the one side, as Parton said, "nearly all the ancient wealth, nearly all the business activity, nearly all the book-nourished intelligence, nearly all the silver-forked civilization of the country." Noting this cleavage and the abandonment of the Democratic Party by its old leaders and its men of talent and wealth, Bryan exclaimed: "At last we have the line drawn, so that a man can take his place on one side or the other." Upon his side, it seemed literally as if there were only "the common people."

V

Full of hope and joy, yet bearing himself everywhere with marked poise, moderation, and courtesy, the Boy Orator proceeded from Chicago to his home in Nebraska in mid-July. The aura of a dramatic national fame hung over him. At railroad stations of every town and village along the way immense throngs came to do honor to the newly risen hero; banners waved and flowers were strewn for him. The people burst through windows or climbed upon telegraph poles to see him and cheer him. "To the excited crowds who pressed about him," wrote the historian Woodrow Wilson at the time, "he seemed a sort of knight errant going about to redress the wrongs of a nation."

Yet after the long procession of what passed for "statesmen" since the Civil War, was it surprising that the young Bryan engendered enthusiasm in the masses? He had given noble voice to their anger and to their hopes. Consciously or unconsciously, Bryan, in his great hour, introduced a new democratic spirit, wanting in our political life since the historic debates and campaigns of Lincoln.

He had the advantage of surprise. His magnetic power over crowds suggested at once to his advisers, as to his own temperament, the scheme of a vigorous, unconventional, even theatrical personal canvass. He would "go to the people" up and down the land, to as many as possible, in a speaking tour such as no one had attempted before, but which the speed and convenience of the modern railroad now permitted.

With his sheer youthful strength and tireless voice, Bryan rivaled the effect of the modern radio broadcasts as he journeyed some 18,000 miles, made over six hundred speeches within three months, and addressed in person over 5,000,000 listeners. It was a circuslike performance; it was also unprecedented, since tradition held that the candidate for the highest office in the land must dissemble his wish for that honor, and appear not to seek the office overtly.

The prodigious pilgrimage by railroad began in the first week of August when the Democratic candidate, instead of receiving formal notification of his nomination at home, set forth to make his speech of acceptance in New York, "the heart of the enemy's country." Here Bryan, reading a carefully prepared address at Madison Square Garden, before 20,000 persons, exhorted them to join with him in the campaign of "the struggling people" against "the money-owning and money-changing class." He had thought to attack the intellect rather than the heart of New York. His long elucidation of the doctrine of bimetallism was probably less effective when read than would have been an emotional exhibition such as he had given at Chicago. Opposition newspapers announced that his "invasion" had fallen flat, that his argument was unconvincing, while a friendly one noted "whirlwinds of enthusiasm" among the electorate. The streets leading to his hotel were blocked by thousands of New Yorkers; to pass through, he was compelled repeatedly to make impromptu addresses to them from his carriage.

In the hostile territory east of the Alleghenies, Bryan was disposed to speak softly. He sought to assure his audience that he was neither a "wild revolutionary" nor a socialist. "Distinctions" of wealth and education, he held with Andrew Jackson, would always exist.

Our campaign has not for its object the reconstruction of society. We cannot insure to the vicious the fruits of a virtuous life . . . we do not propose to transfer the rewards of industry to the lap of indolence. Property is and will remain the stimulus to endeavor and the compensation for toil.

But, he closed, when great aggregations of wealth were trespassing upon the rights of individuals, the time had come to ignore those who had a "pecuniary" interest in noninterference, and to take action.

The new leader of the Democratic Party on this occasion also formed a friendly alliance with Tammany Hall, saying: "Great is Tammany! And Croker is its prophet!" Bryan never affected a horror of simple, patronage-seeking politicians. The shrewd boss of New York's

proletarian voters, for his part, could not appear to resist the glamorous candidate of his party, though Tammany's organizing power was permitted this year to be less prominent than its enthusiasm.

During August, Bryan launched his campaign in earnest. Night after night he rolled across the country, prayed to his God kneeling on the floor of his sleeping-car, slept soundly, and arose refreshed to address himself, during twenty or thirty halts, to as many as 100,000 persons in a day. He spoke spontaneously, with his wonted earnestness and power, and often with native wit. To the crowds he appeared "godlike" as he placed himself at the head of the greatest rising of the poorer classes and the equally numerous middle classes which the country had ever known.

From his train platform, vividly and with abandon, before crowds of Ohio hog farmers or wheat-growers in Illinois (the "Sucker State") he would paint the evils of mortgage foreclosures. He would exclaim: "It is because your legislation has been making the farmer's life harder all the time; it is because the non-producing classes have been producing the laws." At St. Paul, Minnesota, the principality of Jim Hill, he attacked railroad-wreckers and Coal Barons who exacted tribute from every fireside, "from those who desire to be protected from the cold of winter." Then in the towns he addressed himself to the merchants and the millers, asserting that with the silver dollar, the great flour magnate would "get nearly twice as many of such dollars for his product and . . . pay wages that will buy as much as the wages paid today and still make as much profit as he does now." To businessmen in general he preached deliverance from the tyranny of the banks. Before city laborers, in great industrial centers such as Chicago, he assailed the monopoly-ridden

Government, which used armed force in strikes; denounced government by injunction (which trade-unions now fought as their greatest danger); advocated the direct income tax upon wealth, recently barred by the Supreme Court.

Rumors of attempted intimidation among workmen were rife, and Bryan advised them openly to conceal their intentions, as was lawful, under the secret ballot: to hold their jobs and march in Republican parades if commanded to do so, but to vote according to their convictions.

As a figure of American politics, Bryan has been charged with failing to make an "all-class combination of the type so frequently effected by Theodore Roosevelt" and so frequently effective in our party life today, while appealing instead to disparate groups and sections and especially those of the agrarians, labor, and the lower middle-class. Where a Theodore Roosevelt endeavored to neutralize important factions among the big capitalists, while attacking others, Bryan — if we except the friendly Silver Cabal, with its limited resources — certainly seems to clash with all enterprises of the larger type and the greater bosses of the East identified with them. He seems to bring down all their concerted, unmitigated hostility. Yet careful reading of his speeches shows that he himself had no coherent class program — wished for no naked "class struggle" — but shifted his emphasis, in turn, to attract highly diverse groups, ranging from the religious, rural pietists to the merchants and organized laborers of the towns.

In general he expounded the notion that the free coinage of silver would increase the circulation of capital and the redistribution of wealth: "When there is more money in circulation there is a better chance for each man to get money than there is when money is scarce."

But to intelligent laborers it seemed doubtful that all their ills would be removed with the revaluation of the gold standard. As one Socialist spokesman, De Leon, said, there was no little fear that labor might be crucified anew "upon a cross of silver." Yet Bryan's assaults upon the "money power" carried conviction; the party platform opposing court injunctions was designed to win over organized city labor. Eugene Debs, like Samuel Gompers of the American Federation of Labor, stumped vigorously for the silver crusade; and from Chicago, embittered by economic strife, Hanna's Republican agents reported:

The labor organizations are against us to a man. Impossible to teach them. They are more interested in the question of Federal jurisdiction over strikes than the money question.

Whether or no Bryan willed or foresaw the outcome, it was a militant mass, ever rising in numbers, that followed him, formed of groups geographically and socially diverse, having in common chiefly the fact that they were groups "out of the center of control and striving to make themselves more effective in the national . . . political life." The people marched and sang revolutionary hymns, and even offered violence to the opposition; in certain large cities — in Chicago, and even in New Haven — adherents of Bryan, roused to a dangerous pitch, stoned Republican Sound Money paraders.

Among the marching crowds in that torrid summer of 1896, the legend of the "Great Commoners" as the embodiment of earlier American ideals of democracy was created, to endure for many years. As he toured the country, an innovator of modern mass leadership, hostile newspapers accused Bryan of a want of dignity unfitting him for the office of President. He replied in a manner which convinced and delighted his followers:

. . . I would rather have it said that I lacked dignity than . . . that I lack backbone to meet the enemies of the Government who work against its welfare in Wall street. What other Presidential candidates did they ever charge with lack of dignity? (*A voice:* "Lincoln.") Yes, my friends, they said it of Lincoln. (*A voice:* "Jackson.") Yes, they said it of Jackson. (*A voice:* "And Jefferson.") Yes, and of Jefferson; he was lacking in dignity too.

The peregrinations of the young Tribune of the People through the older Middle West to the Northwest, as far as the highest Rockies, and back to the Southern "border" States and Chicago, created a mobile democratic forum by which the masses felt themselves engaged directly in a discussion of the Burning Questions of the day. The price of wheat and corn, the cost of mortgage debt and crop loans, the need for regulating railroads and industrial corporations, for curbing our Supreme Court, for leveling the inequalities of wealth by an income tax — all these immediate (rather than partisan or fictive) issues were agitated day by day in the continuous and vast democratic symposium which the champion of the silver dollar conducted.

By such novel methods, astounding the professional politicians, the masses of the people were directly reached everywhere; enormous forces of sympathy, of fraternal emotion, of hope, were stirred as in a great "democratic debauch" or folk festival. It was an effort worthy of a more certain and clear-visioned leadership, a more rational program of social reorganization than mere unaided monetary inflation which — after its interval of economic confusion — would have left all social re-

lations of property, all sources of inequality, unaltered.

Meanwhile, the storm blew hard over the country. In September the professional politicians who knew how to measure popular trends were in despair. Yet keener minds among them, like Hanna's, noted that Bryan promised too much: "He's talking Silver all the time." He promised by silver inflation an improved distribution of wealth. There were glaring fallacies in the claims of this "Christian Statesman" who believed simply that "the great political questions are in the last analysis moral questions"; and it was upon these weaknesses that the heaviest attacks were centered.

VI

Democrats or Republicans, the big capitalists and the rentier class were agreed upon the common end they had in view; they were moreover terribly determined. Yet their unaided votes alone might well prove insufficient for the battle at the polls. The first field reports in late July and August, attesting to the Great Commoner's popularity, caused pessimism to run rampant in Republican circles for several weeks, as Mr. Hanna arrived in New York to take charge of the national campaign.

History is made of classes and economic forces in conflict; but history, as all recognize, is also full of heroes and fools who serve for a moment to impede or divert the stream of events or hasten the solution of a foredoomed crisis. Bryan was a voice and, in a sense, an American conscience who gave freer reign to the discontent and impulses of the Have-Nots, lending them an ethico-religious ("fundamentalist") and sectional form. But Mark Hanna was a political generalissimo of genius, risen suddenly from the councils of the leading capitalists, to meet and checkmate the drive of the masses by summoning up the beserk fighting power latent in his class. John Hay wrote now to a friend in Paris:

I never knew Mark Hanna intimately until we went into this fight together, but my esteem and admiration for him have grown every hour. . . . He is a born general in politics, perfectly square, honest and courageous, with a *coup d'oeil* for the battle-field and a knowledge of the enemy's weak points which is very remarkable.

The financial metropolis saw him go to work at once at the Eastern national headquarters (which he established, wisely enough, in the building of the Metropolitan Life Insurance Company), and was soon able to measure the brusque force, the "iron will" of this "plain Western business man." No sooner was he off the train than he was in touch with everything and everyone; he was seen ordering supplies and "literature," making appointments, arranging conferences with the veteran politicians, Platt of the New York hierarchy, Quay (a constant counselor), Redfield Proctor of Vermont, Fassenden of Connecticut, Joseph Manley of Maine, all of the national committeemen who could be reached. Hanna's energy and resolution compelled confidence and respect. "You make me think of a lot of scared hens," he is said to have exclaimed to a group of pessimistic capitalists at the Union League Club.

In a sense — and his craftiness here can scarcely be underestimated—Hanna actually exploited the prevailing pessimism. Bryan was absurd, but the farmers swallowed his fallacies and there was a tremendous work to be done; it would be madness to shirk it or miscalculate it. As he moved with Mr. Cornelius Bliss among the groups of bankers, industrialists, and insurance-company magnates, he unfolded the plan of his "educational campaign," involving a direct canvass (paralleling Bryan's vast effort) of the voters in every town and hamlet of thirty Northern States. This would need far more money than anyone had ever conceived of as needed for a political campaign. To parody the famous words of Danton upon the need of boldness in revolution, Hanna frankly said to the American capitalists in 1896: What we need is money, more money, and still more money. A Republican leader wrote to William Beer, the lawyer for the New York Life Insurance Company:

I wish that Hanna would not talk so freely about money. But I know that we are going to need more. It is disappointing that a Democrat like McCall [president of the New York Life Insurance Company] has more sense of the real situation than Mr. Depew [president of the New York Central Railroad].

But at the Union League Club Mr. Hanna continued to preach to the New York capitalists the need for "three million more dollars for the campaign fund," and for thousands of speakers, brass bands, and educational pamphlets on Sound Money by the ton. Not only Republicans, but many an affluent Democrat, such as Cleveland's former Secretary of the Treasury Charles Fairchild, and the shipping magnate W. R. Grace, were seen by newspapermen conferring with Hanna at his headquarters. The financiers were consternated; Hanna exacted almost as much money as they might lose to Bryan! A million or two had been enough previously; but now there was private talk, apparently, of $10,000,000 or $15,000,000, colossal sums such as no political leader had ever before been trusted with.

When Mark Hanna left for the West in August, he had made a good beginning, but bewilderment and fright still ruled in the East. At Western headquarters in Chicago, which was to be the real front for the field workers, trusted Hanna lieutenants such as Charles G. Dawes, Charles Dick, and W. M. Hahn and Henry C. Payne of Wisconsin were placed in charge of the work.

Hanna set up a complete machinery for modern political warfare. The Republican National Committee, which he headed, instead of being a sort of clearinghouse, a kind of central agency (chiefly for receiving appeals for funds from State bosses worried about their districts), became the general staff of the whole army. Its orders were carried out by the State committees automatically, as if they were the branch offices of one of the modern, centralized industrial Trusts in oil, steel, or sugar. A loose confederation of Republican regional leaders and ward heelers was whipped into the shape of a machinelike army, under a single leader who oversaw everything, who infused all its men, from top to bottom, with his confidence and resolution.

At Canton, Hanna arranged also a careful program with the amiable Major McKinley, who, the reader must bear in mind, was still the candidate for the Presidency. McKinley, a student for many years of the blunders of Blaine, Hancock, Harrison, and other candidates of his generation, was a master of the mot juste. He would make no break in public over some chance phrase such as "rum, Romanism and rebellion," but planned all details in advance. The Boy Orator might tour the country and make his one speech twice or ten times a day, but Mr. McKinley would keep his ingratiating personality before the public as much as Bryan — by remaining at home. McKinley

and Hanna carefully plotted their celebrated "front-porch" tactics, by which large organized delegations of editors, ministers, prominent citizens, war veterans, temperance societies, Presbyterians, farmers, railroad workers, wholesale merchants, Catholics, Germans, Negroes, like so many trained seals, with their expenses paid in advance, were induced to make pilgrimages to the home of the Napoleon of Canton, Ohio. There the visitors gazed upon their candidate, paid him honor, and asked him certain leading questions of the day (as written out beforehand by the McKinley staff), and received from him a gracious welcome and a prepared answer, which was forthwith published by the press of the nation.

The front porch in Canton became a national sounding-board. It is related that the leaders of proposed delegations would announce their intention to New York headquarters or to McKinley, or even come on a preliminary visit. McKinley would then say: "You are going to represent the delegation and make some remarks. What are you going to say?" Any old thing? That would scarcely do, and might be gravely inconvenient. McKinley would then ask to see the address in advance, censor it, and send it back in the form he desired. In one case at least, a speech was blue-penciled twice over and virtually dictated by the candidate, so that it had the precise effect desired "from the party's standpoint," as McKinley expressed it.

The mock ceremony would take place at the appointed time, one, ten, or twenty a day. McKinley would come forth in all his dignity, with his round decent paunch, his unruffled white vest and cutaway, and a conventional politician's black hat; he would shake hands, smile warmly as he knew how to smile, and burst into "spontaneous" oration in answer to his guests:

. . . this year is going to be a year of patriotism and devotion to country. I am glad to know that the people in every part of the country mean to be devoted to one flag, and that the glorious Stars and Stripes (great applause); that the people of the country this year mean to maintain the financial honor of the country as sacredly as they maintain the honor of the flag.

What we want, no matter to what political organization we may have belonged in the past, is a return to the good times of years ago. We want good prices and good wages and when we have them we want them to be paid in good money . . . in dollars worth one hundred cents each.

With an air of the most unctuous patriotism, McKinley, the Civil War veteran, attacked the suggestion of sectional strife raised by his opponent, saying: "We know no 'enemy's country' in this fair land of ours." Nor did he neglect, as usual, to repeat his old familiar appeals to American workmen; he extolled the "dignity of labor," and gave dire warnings of the consequences of a "cheap dollar" for wage-earners. Finally, his addresses emphasized ever and again the destructive class antagonisms stirred up by the Silver Democrats. "In America," he said, "we spurn all class distinctions. We are all equal citizens and equal in privilege and opportunity."

This front-porch game was played all summer and fall at increasing tempo. After having ordered immense quantities of engravings of his friend William labeled: "The Advance Agent of Prosperity," Mark Hanna returned on August 15 to his labors over the supply problem behind the front in New York.

Meanwhile Bryan was stumping through western New York and the nearby Middle West. McKinley will lose Ohio! observers predicted. Panic rose; gold was being hoarded or exported; stocks had sinking spells; and money was wanting still for the trainloads of pamphlets and the exhaustive canvass which Hanna designed in all its detail, with agents penetrating into every election district. The period from mid-August to early September, when the advance "sixty-day" polls were taken, was the low ebb of Republican hopes. Hanna's second visit to the East "is being wholly devoted to getting funds," the press gossiped. It was at this point that James J. Hill came East from his railroad headquarters in St. Paul to join his efforts with those of Mr. Hanna and Cornelius Bliss, treasurer of the Republican National Committee.

Hill, coming fresh from the frenzied Northwest of Commonwealers and Populists and Silverites, conducted Hanna promptly to the "high places" of Wall Street. During the week of August 15, the press noted daily the progress of the carriage containing Mr. Hill and Mr. Hanna, uptown and downtown, from Wall Street to the Pennsylvania Railroad offices, and to the New York Central offices. At the House of Morgan, at Kuhn, Loeb's, Hill corroborated Hanna's testimony as to the reality of the danger threatened; it was not a politician's scare for the sake of making free with the banker's money, but an emergency. Hanna could be trusted to use to the full political donations, unlike professionals who by common report wasted half the sums given them. Hill, who had bought large quantities of coal for the Great Northern Railroad from Hanna, vouched for his friend's integrity. Thus there came into use, in greatly expanded form, the device of the *political assessment upon corporate wealth* used in 1888.

After these mad cab rides of Jim Hill and Mark Hanna up and down New York, the morale of the Republican army improved wonderfully. "The feeling about

Mr. Hanna has changed," writes one of the general staff from the field of action. "He has made a lot of these people see that he knows what he is doing. But there is a bad scare here."

Once again "Dollar-Mark" Hanna's contribution to American political science has the stamp of genius and fresh invention, carrying further, perfecting, tendencies and devices partly used or foreshadowed. Working in Ohio under the orders of Matt Quay in the famous boodle and "fat-frying" campaign of 1888, Hanna had studied well the handiwork of a master, had become himself adept in the "little shows of sharp practice and most of the big schemes of fine politics now in use by the Republican National Committee." But instead of appealing to or wheedling the protected manufacturers who were privileged by the tariff subsidy, Hanna organized thoroughly the business of collecting contributions on the ground that the very life of business and credit was at stake. Responsible men were appointed to act as local agents in all the large cities, soliciting and receiving funds.

Mr. Hanna always did his best to convert the practice of fund-raising from a matter of political begging on the one side and donating on the other into a matter of systematic assessment according to the means of the individual and institution. In the case of the banks and trust companies a regular assessment was levied, calculated . . . at the rate of one-quarter of one per cent of their capital, and this assessment was for the most part paid.

The Standard Oil (admitting a valuation now of $100,000,000), through Mr. Archbold and William Rockefeller, who knew Hanna well, turned in $250,000; J. P. Morgan did likewise; the four great meat-packing houses of Chicago were reported to have given altogether $400,000. Mr.

McCall, of the New York Life Insurance Company, was called upon again and again. George W. Perkins, both a Morgan partner and an insurance-company officer, and William H. Hyde of the great Equitable company testified some years later (in the Hughes investigation) that they gave freely large portions of their clients' premiums toward aiding the Republican campaign of 1896. This was equivalent to a bank's giving up part of its depositors' money for a political campaign.

Thus a war chest equal to all demands was gathered by Hanna, a sum which Croly modestly estimates at $3,500,000 (as officially recorded), but which other estimates have placed at from $10,000,000 to $16,500,000. Never had politicians wallowed in such a golden stream as now poured forth for them, and which increased in abundance up to the closing days.

The printing of 120,000,000 copies of 275 different pamphlets in English, German, Italian, Polish, Yiddish, Greek, Swedish, and other languages was pushed forward, and their distribution in carlots organized. The speeches of McKinley, Thomas Reed, John Sherman, and John Hay were broadcast to the millions. Willing academicians also, such as J. Lawrence Laughlin of the Rockefeller-endowed University of Chicago, were hired for the occasion and painted the uncertainties of monetary inflation in the darkest colors. All arguments were pointed to a concrete appeal to people of small means: first, upon the question of the future purchasing power of the dollar; second, upon the immediate effect of silver inflation on savings, pensions, insurance, and small investments.

Nor did the high command of the Republican campaign halt at provoking the most violent class hate. Aggressive young

Republican orators, such as Henry Cabot Lodge and Theodore Roosevelt, then the Police Commissioner of New York, and even respectable ministers of the church, attempted to outdo with their billingsgate firebrands like Tillman. Altgeld was chosen as the main target of attack; he was "the crowned hero and worshipped deity of the anarchists of the Northwest," who used the pliable Bryan as his pawn, said Dr. Lyman Abbott. On October 16, 1896, before a crowd of 15,000 in Altgeld's own city of Chicago, Theodore Roosevelt, who this season distinguished himself as a picturesque stump orator, characterized the Governor of Illinois as "one who condones and encourages the most infamous of murders," and "would substitute for the government of Washington and Lincoln . . . a red government of lawlessness and dishonesty as fantastic and vicious as the Paris Commune. . . . Bryan . . . would steal from the creditors of the nation half of what they have saved." The sophisticated John Hay delivered himself of a coldly conceived piece of vituperation entitled "The Platform of Anarchy," which was broadcast by the Eastern press; while more innocent personages, such as Dr. Charles H. Parkhurst of New York, also pointed their fire upon the menace of "anarchy" raised by the reform projects of Bland, Altgeld, and Bryan.

It was not the first time that the cry of "anarchy" had been raised in America against levelers and egalitarians. This constituted, in fact, tried and tested tactics. Under Washington and Hamilton the Federalists had wielded such arms fiercely against Jefferson's Democratic-Republicans; later, in the 1830's, Clay and the men of the United States Bank had raised a similar alarm against the Jacksonians. Now again the hue and cry was raised against the new Jacobins and their program of "chaos and cupidity," their promises of "boodle" to farmer, laborer, and miner. American political discussion was as traditionally given to violence of pre-election epithet as the people were given to post-election respect for the laws and peaceable behavior. One wonders sometimes what epithets would be employed for a truly radical political movement designed to eliminate a large portion of existing privilege.

While appealing to historic tradition and "principle," Republican Party strategy itself did not ignore the immediate appeal of "boodle." In addition to the circulation of colored lithographs of McKinley, bearing a Full Dinner Pail and entitled "The Advance Agent of Prosperity," a sudden and rather mysterious rise in the price of wheat, from 64 cents a bushel in July, to 82 cents in October, was also used to point its moral. "Now do something for corn," said voices from the agricultural States.

Early in September even Hanna had been thoroughly alarmed at learning, through careful private polls, that the sure Republican State of Iowa held some 30,000 "bolters" and with Populist aid would go decisively for Bryan. In this and other "doubtful" States he ordered the most elaborate advance polls, without regard to cost. Through September and half of October Hanna directed his attention upon Iowa and other Granger States; his speakers and "drummers," armed with campaign literature and other "substantial arguments," were sent into every town and village, ordered not to return until the hurrah for Bryan had been converted into a hurrah for McKinley, gold, and Protection. The work was well done. A second private canvass, toward October 15, showed that Iowa was "saved," and Hanna turned to concentrate his attack upon Illinois, Ohio, and Michigan.

Yet new danger appeared in October again when organized labor, spurred by Altgeld and Debs, was shown to be swinging irresistibly toward the Democratic candidate. Roused by inhuman insult and libel, Altgeld came to New York and in a three-hour speech at Cooper Union sought to vindicate his actions in 1894 and the platform of his party. He seemed beside himself with passion, as were so many others in this season of hate. But during his speaking tour none knew of his frequent fainting spells, from which he rose resolutely, at the risk of death from a heart attack, to fight again. Never had he spoken so clearly, so seriously, so tellingly as at New York on October 17, 1896, when the plain people of the city received him with tremendous ovations. It is toil that makes civilization and not the cutting of coupons, he said. "The American people are called on this year to *make a new Declaration of Independence to mankind.*"

On the other hand, during a Republican rally in Brooklyn, Mark Hanna was greeted "like a President," and in response to many noisy, good-humored calls, was finally introduced as the "Warwick of the West." The tall magnate, his face wreathed in smiles, gave a pleasant impromptu talk, in which he said meaningfully: "If I have been successful in anything in this campaign, it is in knowing enough not to talk too much." Hanna's final moves were made without any talk whatsoever.

Under the surface an ugly spirit of coercion and intimidation suddenly showed itself in the late stages of the campaign. For some time agents of the greater insurance companies from New York and Connecticut had gone about quietly informing their debtors that "if McKinley were elected, their mortgages would be extended for five years at a low rate of interest."

But toward the end of September, when Bryan seemed far in the lead, the tactics of more and more direct coercion spread quickly and quite openly — as if by a prearranged signal, one might have said, everywhere, East, West, North — upon a greater scale than ever before in an electoral contest. Large "contingent" orders were sent to iron manufacturers and shipbuilders, with the proviso that they be canceled if Bryan were elected. Gold-payment clauses were written into bank loans. Important employers now came before their workers with gloomy warnings that if McKinley were defeated there would be a dearth of business, their factories would run on half-time or would be shut down entirely for the coming winter. A workingman entered Democratic headquarters in Chicago weeping, and crying aloud for all to hear that he had been threatened with dismissal; his family would starve because he had been a leader in his district Democratic campaign.

In September also some of the railroads began to circularize their employees with printed statements in each pay envelope, warning them that the roads would be ruined if they were compelled to pay bond interest in gold while earning depreciated American money; rolling stock, it was predicted, would come to a standstill everywhere if Bryan were elected.

"Who are these men who are so solicitous about your wages?" ran one of the Democratic circulars in answer. Mr. Carnegie, Mr. Hanna? Had not those gentlemen reduced workingmen's wages and compelled them to accept these reductions by force of police and soldiers?" But the tactics of intimidation were now spreading like a disease.

On October 19, Chairman Jones of the Democratic National Committee made a strong public protest that "the great corporations, with scarcely an exception, and many of the large employers of labor are engaged in a concerted effort to coerce their employees to vote against their convictions. . . . The workingman is being robbed of his 'rights' as an American citizen by an appeal to force and fraud." On October 20, Hanna replied publicly that the accusation was absurd; Republicans, he added cynically, could not possibly resort to such "un-American" measures. He himself would help in tracking down such malefactions if they actually existed.

Two days later, Jones reported that numerous Chicago manufacturers were threatening their workers with dismissal or cuts in wages. He then cleverly advised all employees to petition their masters for guarantees of a raise in wages in the event of McKinley's election. Hanna replied in a vehement outburst on October 24 that the Democrats were the ones using coercive methods in "a bold attempt to excite workmen against their employers."

In the final fortnight, tension grew unbelievably high, especially in centers such as Chicago. Bryan, speaking there on October 28, 1896, for a last time before the balloting, brought the whole city into the streets. From his open carriage he reviewed hundreds of thousands, passing among them as "the incarnation of triumphant revolution," according to the Eastern press. Once more street fighting and rioting broke out in Chicago, where Republican paraders were attacked and McKinley billposters torn from walls and burned. In a Kentucky town the Democratic "traitors" Palmer and Buckner, the Gold Democrat candidates for the Presidency and the Vice-Presidency, were surrounded by a mob and roughly handled. Cities trembled with commotion; families and parishes were divided by hate. Nervous police took special precautions throughout the country as election day approached, especially at New York, where Republicans prepared a monster "victory parade" for Saturday, October 31, preceding the election.

All expert reports now indicated that Mr. Bryan would probably be defeated; but none would guarantee that he might not win. Since mid-October, when the coercive measures had been undertaken in earnest, the game was really up. "It is all over," Hanna wrote confidently on October 28 to a friend who had contributed a check, which he returned. "Reports are satisfactory just where we wanted them most." Two days before, the dependable Boss Cox of Cincinnati had reported a complete reversal in "doubtful" Ohio. The systematic tactics of coercion applied everywhere, added to the dragnet which swept every tiny rural community for floaters or possible added votes, had completed the task.

On the Saturday evening before election, Democratic headquarters at Chicago, where hope for victory still ran strong, were startled by a press dispatch announcing that the leading railroads and the great manufacturers had determined upon a final united ultimatum to their employees for Monday, November 2, to the effect that none need return to work if Bryan were elected.

"Men, vote as you please," the head of the Steinway piano works is reported to have said, in terms which were repeated throughout the country, "but if Bryan is elected tomorrow the whistle will not blow Wednesday morning."

An excited discussion arose among the Democratic leaders, Jones and Teller among them, as to what was to be done on the instant. Some present held that this final shameless "un-American" threat would serve as a boomerang, since it would be secretly resented. But the venerable Senator Teller shook his head sadly and said: "Boys, I am afraid it beats us. If I were a working man and had nothing but my job, I am afraid when I came to vote I would think of Mollie and the babies."

The highly organized Sound Money parade and victory demonstration by the Republicans at New York, on October 31, included by most estimates 150,000 people and was witnessed by perhaps 1,000,000 more. All that Saturday afternoon and all evening, while the city was brilliantly illuminated and bedecked, the marchers with tin horns and flags, wearing costumes or riding in floats, filled the streets. As before, trade associations, moving in battalions, with banners marking them as wine and spirit dealers, or lawyers, or railroad officials, sang songs in the characteristic vernacular of the time. Thus the railroad men:

> Hully-gee! Who are we?
> Erie! E--ee--rie!

The stockbrokers and bank clerks passing before the Union League Club cheered and shouted: "We want Morgan!" The final mass meeting of the Democratic Party, too, was an occasion for speeches, fireworks, and celebrations up to a late hour, until the great city, strewn with rubbish, broken papier-mâché, colored bunting, and campaign buttons, sank to sleep in exhaustion.

In the last hour's preparations for "getting out the vote," for rounding up the floaters all over the country and in all closely disputed regions, nothing had been overlooked by Mr. Hanna's superb Organization. Moral enthusiasm was to be beaten at every point in the line by a machinelike domination of the actual polling. This department had been prepared by Mr. Hanna and his aides for weeks in advance, and its storming parties waited impatiently for their hour. In some thousand precincts the Republican district leaders and their henchmen were provided for by a last distribution of gold pieces. As one veteran political journalist related, every person having a vehicle on wheels was hired to transport voters from their homes to election booths and back:

> Voters who were at work and possibly subject to loss of time while going to the election were paid for their time, many of them upon a very liberal basis. Farmers who had to leave their fields were recompensed for their loss of time and for the loss of time of their hired hands. . . . Every voter, no matter in what condition he may have been, was sought out. . . . Every county chairman, district chairman, precinct captain . . . lieutenants, and all other willing workers, were supplied with money to get out the votes.

In Ohio there was one vote cast for every four living persons (with women then not voting), surpassing all previous records by 25 per cent. In Indiana there were 30,000 floaters reported by watchers as receiving besides sandwiches and liquor only $5 a head in this year of depression. The Democratic district captains in Indiana, according to their leaders, suffered from a lack of "political mechanics" to handle the vote, and stood by watching helplessly. In one Western district having only 30,000 registered voters some 48,000 voted, by an oversight of Mr. Hanna's men. Reports of Negroes imported by trainloads across Mason and Dixon's line were heard at many points. "The very graveyards were robbed of the names on their tombstones."

The Democratic Party funds, finally, which were officially estimated at $425,000, were countered with a Republican war chest probably ten times greater, and unofficially reckoned at twenty or thirty times greater.

The leaders of the reborn Democratic Party, as they measured the sweep of the early returns, realized, as Altgeld said, that while they had been able to make "the most heroic political fight ever seen," the odds had been too great. The Party, Altgeld said, was

confronted by all the banks, all the trusts, all the syndicates, all the corporations, all the great papers. It was confronted by everything that money could buy, that boodle could debauch, or that fear of starvation could coerce. . . . It was confronted by a combination of forces such as had never been united before and will probably never be united again; and worse still, the time was too short to educate the public.

An enormous vote had been brought forth, the greatest outpouring in our history, of which Bryan — "repudiation," "anarchy" and all — had nearly 6,500,000 (more than had ever before voted for a President), while McKinley had some 7,000,000. The Republican electoral majority, however, was decisive, standing at 271 to 176. But the change of 14,000 votes, it has been estimated, distributed in six States (some of which were carried by but a few hundred votes)— California, Oregon, Kentucky, Indiana, North Dakota, and West Virginia — would have yielded a clear Democratic-Populist victory. The supreme importance of Hanna's strategy and dynamic Organization was thus proved beyond a doubt.

"God's in his Heaven, all's right with the world!" Mr. Hanna telegraphed to his friend, William, who knelt and prayed for joy in his bedroom at Canton. Mr. Hanna

had made a President, and prepared for a long reign in which there would be gold and privilege, protective tariffs high enough for the most ambitious of manufacturers, and in consequence a Full Dinner Pail for contented, submissive labor. The nightmare of Altgeld as a power in the country was ended. And Bryan, as the New York *Tribune* thundered,

the wretched, rattle-pated boy, posing in vapid vanity and mouthing his resounding rottenness . . . goes down with the cause and must abide with it in the history of infamy. . . . Good riddance to it all . . . to the foul menace of repudiation and Anarchy against the honor and life of the Republic.

Mr. Bryan, to be sure, was not to pass his life "abiding in infamy," but became instead the idol of Western Democracy, and for almost two decades his party's dominant leader. The silver question vanished with the increase of gold production in 1896 and 1900 and the approach to "elastic" currency under a central banking system. The Democratic Party, having lost completely the favor of "the big bankers, the big manufacturers, the big masters of commerce," under Bryan, wandered in the wilderness of defeat for long years, as had been predicted; it was long a minority party of opposition, supported normally by Bryan's Western agrarians, the Solid South, and an aggregation of professional city machines in the Northeast. In their voting, city laborers certainly showed no decided preference for the Democratic Party, especially during the years of Theodore Roosevelt, who took lessons from the Boy Orator in mass leadership. Thus the farmer-labor class alignment, which made 1896 so dramatic, disappeared, and the great parties reverted to type, on the whole resuming their old character of identical parts within our traditional party institution. This status held good after the upheavals of the "New Freedom" under President Wilson, 1912–16, as after the social upheavals over silver, 1893–96, thus revealing the amazing persistence and strength of the institution. Its greatest test came undoubtedly with the profound depression of the 1930's and the class alignments of 1936.

But on November 4, 1896, the men who carried on in the Republican Party the essentially unchanged tradition of Hamilton and Webster, seeing in themselves the triumph of "wealth and talents," apparently glimpsed something of the scope of their victory, the long years of unchallenged sway, the glittering opportunities before them and, humanly enough, "let joy be unconfined."

When the returns of November 3 indicated McKinley's certain election, in a certain Chicago club, long after midnight,

one of the world's greatest merchants started the boyhood game of "Follow the Leader." He was joined by bank presidents, merchants, Chicago's foremost men; they went over sofas, chairs, tables, up-stairs and down-stairs, and wound up with dancing in each other's arms.

And in this agreeable humor of their great hour we may charitably leave our Republican friends, facing strange years of war and peace, growth and change.

Herbert Croly: THE CAMPAIGN OF 1896

WHEN Mr. Hanna was selected as chairman of the Republican National Committee, no one anticipated how grave and difficult his task would be. As I have said, the action of the Democratic Convention took the country by surprise and completely upset the calculations and plans of the Republican leaders. They had never suspected that the currency issue, even if made decisive, would entirely supersede the tariff issue. They never anticipated that by virtue of the currency issue the Democrats would be able to make political capital out of a period of economic privation, which had been appropriated for the political benefit of the Republicans and particularly of Mr. McKinley. A few weeks before the Republican Convention it looked like plain sailing for the Republican nominee. A week after the Democratic Convention it looked as if by sheer audacity and misguided enthusiasm the Democrats had obtained the right of way, and that the Boy Orator would be carried into the White House on a flood of popular discontent.

In July, 1896, no one could gauge accurately the actual range and force of this discontent. No one could estimate how far its ignorance could be enlightened or its impetus diverted. No one could tell with any confidence what effect Mr. Bryan's gallant and strenuous appeal to the American people would have upon

Herbert Croly, *Marcus Alonzo Hanna* (New York: The Macmillan Company, 1912), pp. 209–227. Used by permission.

the actual vote. But the extreme gravity of the situation was manifest. Many of the men most familiar with the situation believe that if the election had been held in August, or even in September, the Democratic candidate would have triumphed. Mr. Hanna himself inclined to this opinion. Mr. McKinley was gravely concerned, and chided certain of his friends for their participation in the decisive definition of the currency issue. In order to save the situation enormous exertions would be required, as well as a plan of campaign for which there was as little precedent as there was for the situation itself.

What took the Republican leaders by surprise was the peculiar effect on popular sentiment of the prevailing hard times. For some reason the business depression, coincident with Mr. Cleveland's second administration, stirred the American people more deeply and had graver political consequences than had any previous economic famine. The panics of 1837, 1873 and perhaps even of 1857 had caused as much, if not more, suffering and privation as did the panic of 1893. The effect, for instance, of the panic of 1873 upon the prevailing rate of wages was more depressing than was the effect of the panic of 1893. But in the earlier years the political consequences were not serious or dangerous. The result in 1837 was the subsequent election of a Whig in place of a Democratic administration. The result in 1873 was the subsequent capture by the opposing party of the House of Representatives and Democratic plurality of the popular vote in the presidential campaign of 1876. On each of these occasions, also, local economic heresies jumped to the surface in the Middle and Far West. But in neither case did these local economic heresies wax into a national issue and become a grave na-

tional peril. In neither case did it result in a campaign in which one of the great political parties declared that the effect of the prevailing economic system was to discriminate in favor of the possessor of loanable capital, and against the borrower, the wage-earner and the producer. The fact that so threatening an economic issue could be nationalized indicated the ebullition of unsuspected forces in American public opinion.

The public opinion of the time, confused and ill-informed as it was, saw one truth very plainly, which was that the cause of the trouble lay deeper than the administration of a Democratic President and the passage of the Wilson Bill. It turned in the beginning instinctively toward Mr. Bryan because he provided the people with an apparently better reason for their privations and a more immediately effective cure. They felt vaguely that some essential economic force was operating to deprive them of the share of economic goods to which they were accustomed; and it was both plausible and comforting to attribute that malevolent power to the men who controlled the money of the country. Thus it came to pass that Mr. Bryan's speeches inevitably assumed more and more the character of appeals to a class interest, and this was just the aspect of the matter which so puzzled and alarmed his adversaries. Not since the campaign against the National Bank, had any issue arisen which encouraged loose talk about the "Money Power" and which made the poor feel that the rich were becoming fat at their expense.

Fortunately, however, Mr. Bryan was appealing to and representing, not merely a class, but a sectional interest. For reasons already indicated, the economic dearth had caused the utmost suffering and privation among the farmers of the second tier of states west of the Mississippi. These people had gone heavily into debt upon the basis of expectations which had been frustrated by poor crops, low prices and the disturbed condition of credit. They turned willingly towards a change in the currency system which might provide them with cheaper money. But there was no reason why the desire for cheaper money should appeal either to farmers who were relatively prosperous, or to the wage-earners in the industries of the country. After the first burst of enthusiasm had been spent over a candidate and a platform which made a strong bid for popular sympathy, there was a fair chance that the more prevalent interests opposed to cheap money would assert themselves. The one thing necessary was to establish clearly and to popularize the real meaning of the demand for the free coinage of silver and the real necessity of an assured standard of value. It would be the fault of the Republicans themselves in case a purely sectional interest were allowed to obtain a national following without having its false pretensions exposed.

The manifest duty of the Republican National Committee was that of explaining fully to the voters the meaning of the Democratic platform and convincing them of its palpable error. It was confronted, that is, literally and exclusively, by a campaign of education, or better of instruction. We hear a great deal about campaigns of education, in many of which the people who need and get the education are the people who run the campaign. But in this particular case a confused and hesitating mass of public opinion merely needed elementary instruction. The prevailing popular discontent was receiving a well-intentioned but erroneous economic expression. A sectional economic interest was demanding a change in the currency system, which from the point of

view of sound economics was entirely and inexcusably wrong. Unlike the controversy between free trade and protection, it was not a matter of two divergent economic policies, each of which expressed under certain conditions a valid political interest and a sound economic truth. It was a matter of undermining by thorough discussion and explanation the foundations of a dangerous and obvious mistake.

Mark Hanna and the other Republican leaders soon understood the kind of campaign work which the situation demanded. They decided to oppose Mr. Bryan's personal appeal to the American people with an exhaustive and systematic educational canvass of the country. There was no hesitation and doubt as to the kind of strategy needed. The difficulty consisted in collecting, organizing, equipping and distributing among its proper fields of action a large enough army to carry out the strategic plan. The prevalence of the heresy, the confusion of public opinion, the uncertainty as to the actual force of the Democratic candidate's personal appeal, and the general obliteration of the usual signposts and land-marks made it necessary to cover an enormously extended territory with operations devised to meet both the local and the general needs of the situation.

In previous campaigns the National Committee could count upon certain states as indubitably Republican and certain other states as indubitably Democratic. Only the appearance of a fight had to be made in such neighborhoods. The real work was done in half a dozen doubtful states, and the Committee could plan with some assurance the methods necessary to secure the best results within these areas. In 1896 all this was changed. Of course some states could still be placed indubitably in one column or the other, and there were a few states, ordinarily doubtful, which were sure to cast their vote either for the golden-mouthed or the silver-tongued candidate. But no one knew where certain parts of the West stood. The Middle West, the Far West and the Pacific Coast were all more or less in doubt. The result was that instead of a campaign carried on in a few dubious states, the field of action was enlarged to include half the country; and within this enlarged field of action an unprecedented amount of campaign work had to be accomplished.

The exigencies of the campaign necessitated certain departures from the customary methods of organization. For a number of reasons the work devolved to a much larger extent than usual upon the National Committee. The time was short. An enormous amount of properly correlated work had to be accomplished with the utmost possible efficiency. Since it was to be a campaign of instruction, the educational agencies had to be concentrated upon the areas in which they could do most good, and they had to be supplied with really instructive material. The State Committees could not be trusted with as much responsibility as they had been accustomed to exercise. The National Committee, instead of being a kind of central agency of the State Committees, became the general staff of the whole army. The State Committees carried out its orders. Such was the inevitable effect of a campaign which stirred public opinion as it had not been stirred since the war, and which raised an issue involving not merely the national prosperity, but the national honor and credit.

It was also a result of naming a man like Mark Hanna as the chairman of the Committee. He was not merely the nominal head of the campaign. He was the real leader of the Committee, the real architect of its plans, the real engineer of its machinery and to a certain extent the real source of its energy. In the work of the campaign no one was more intimately associated with him than the treasurer of the Committee, the late Mr. Cornelius N. Bliss, and no one testifies more cordially to his unremitting labor, his unflagging energy, his thorough grasp of the work in all its aspects, his quick insight into the different needs born of different situations and his fertility in meeting special needs with special measures.

As one necessary preliminary measure he reorganized the executive offices of the Committee. In the past its methods had not conformed to sound business standards. Mr. Hanna introduced a better system of bookkeeping and auditing, so that there would be a proper account kept of the way in which the funds of the Committee were spent. Another innovation was the establishment of two headquarters, one in New York and one in Chicago. In the beginning he anticipated that the Eastern office would be the more important, but the large amount of work which was necessitated in the West by the disaffection in that region demanded an independent organization. As the campaign developed, this double-headed organization was justified by the event. Chicago became the real centre of the educational part of the campaign, because of its proximity to the doubtful states.

Mr. Hanna had intended to divide his own attention about equally between the two headquarters, but as the campaign progressed his personal responsibility for raising money to pay the expenses of the Committee kept him a large part of the time in New York. He needed, consequently, a peculiarly efficient local organization in Chicago, and he secured it by associating with him in the work unusually able men. The vice-chairman in charge of the office was Mr. Henry C. Payne of Wisconsin, who is said to be one of the most successful campaign managers of that period. With him was associated Charles G. Dawes, who had proved his abilities in the fight made by McKinley's friends for Illinois, Winfield T. Durbin of Indiana and Cyrus Leland, Jr., of Kansas. The subordinates were all men with whom Mr. Hanna had already worked and in whose abilities he had confidence. Major Charles Dick was secretary to the committee and the working head of the organization. William M. Hahn, formerly chairman of the Ohio State Committee, was in charge of the Bureau of Speakers, and Perry Heath took care of the press matter. In New York, besides Mr. Cornelius N. Bliss, the work was divided among Senator Quay, Joseph Manley of Maine, Powell Clayton of Arkansas and N. B. Scott of West Virginia.

One of the major necessities of the campaign as a whole was the adoption of some measure which would counteract the effect of Mr. Bryan's personal stumping tour, — a tour which covered a large part of the country and aroused a great popular sympathy and interest. Of course the countermove was to keep Mr. McKinley's ingratiating personality as much as possible before the public; but the Republican candidate cherished a high respect for the proprieties of political life and refused to consider a competing tour of his own. It was arranged, consequently, that inasmuch as McKinley could not go to the people, the people must come to McKinley. The latter adjured the stump, but when his supporters paid him a visit, he could address them from his own front porch. This idea was employed and developed to the very limit. Several times a week delegations of loyal Republicans came to Canton from all points of the compass to pay their respects to the candidate. The chairman of the delegation would make a short speech, telling Mr. McKinley a few little truths with which he was already familiar, and Mr. McKinley would answer at smaller or greater length, according to the importance of the delegation or the requirements of the general campaign at that particular juncture. These delegations were not mere committees. They frequently included some thousands of people and had to be carried to Canton in trains of several sections.

It is characteristic both of Mr. Hanna and Mr. McKinley that every detail of these visitations was carefully prearranged. The candidate was not taking any chance of a reference by some alliterative chairman to the party of Silver, Sacerdotalism and Sedition. In the first place, while many of the pilgrimages were the result of a genuine desire on the part of enthusiastic Republicans to gaze upon their candidate, others were deliberately planned by the Committee for the sake of their effect both upon the pilgrims and upon public opinion. But, whether instigated or spontaneous, Mr. McKinley always had to know in advance just what the chairman was going to say. The general procedure was something as follows: A letter would be sent to the National Committee or to Canton, stating that a delegation of farmers, railroad employees, cigar-makers, wholesale merchants, Presbyterians or what-not would, if convenient, call on Mr. McKinley on such a day. An answer would immediately be returned expressing pleasure at the idea, but requesting that the head of the delegation make a preliminary visit to the candidate. When he appeared, Mr. McKinley would greet him warmly and ask: "You are going to represent the delegation and make some remarks. What are you going to say?" The reply would usually be: "Oh! I don't know. Anything that ocurs to me." Then Mr. McKinley would point out the inconveniences of such a course and request that a copy of the address be sent to him in advance, and he usually warned his interlocutor that he might make certain suggestions looking towards the revision of the speech.

In one instance, according to ex-Senator Charles Dick, a man took his speech to Canton, all written out, and at McKinley's request read it aloud to the candidate. After he had finished Mr. McKinley said: "My friend, that is a splendid speech, a magnificent speech. No one could have prepared a better one. There are many occasions on which it would be precisely the right thing to say; but is it quite suitable to this peculiar occasion? Sound and sober as it is from your standpoint, I must consider its effect from the party's standpoint. Now you go home and write a speech along the lines I indicate, and send me a copy of it." In this particular case, even the second version was thoroughly blue-pencilled until it satisfied the exigent candidate. Such a method was not calculated to produce bursts of personal eloquence on the part of the chairman of the delegation, but the candidate preferred himself to provide the eloquence. Knowing as he did in advance just what the chairman would say, his own answer was carefully prepared. He had secretaries to dig up any information he needed, but he always conscientiously wrote out the speech itself. If it were short, he would memorize it. If it were long, he would read it. In consequence, his addresses to the American people during the campaign, beginning with the letter of acceptance, were unusually able and raised him in the estimation of many of his earlier opponents. He made a genuine personal contribution to the discus-

sion of the dominant issue and extorted increasing respect from general public opinion. As the campaign progressed and the strain began to count, Mr. Bryan's speeches deteriorated both in dignity and poignancy, while those of Mr. McKinley maintained an even level of sobriety, pertinence and good sense.

Mr. McKinley was only the leader of an army of speakers who were preaching the same doctrine to the American people. The Republicans had a great advantage over the Democrats in the number of speakers of ability at their disposal, who knew what they were talking about and believed in it. The National Committee took full advantage of their resources. They collected a body of 1400 campaigners, paid their expenses and sent them wherever their services were most needed. In the doubtful states the canvass was most exhaustive and more careful than ever before in the history of the country. The agents of the committee penetrated, wherever necessary, into every election district and held small local meetings. Hand in hand with these meetings went an equally thorough circulation of campaign literature. There are good reasons for believing that this work was really efficient. Early in September, for instance, a careful canvass of Iowa indicated a probable majority for Bryan in that state. During the next six weeks, speakers and campaign documents were poured into every town and village. In October the results of another canvass convinced the Committee that the state was safe for McKinley.

Even more elaborate were the provisions made for the distribution of campaign literature. This feature of the canvass increased in importance as it progressed, and finally attained a wholly unexpected volume and momentum. The greater part of the responsibility fell upon the Chicago headquarters, and this fact made the work performed at Chicago relatively more important than that performed in New York. Over 100,000,000 documents were shipped from the Chicago office, whereas not more than 20,000,000 were sent out from New York. In addition the Congressional Committee at Washington circulated a great deal of printed matter. The material was derived from many sources, — chiefly from Mr. McKinley's own speeches and from those which various congressmen had made at different times on behalf of sound money. A pamphlet of forty pages, dealing with the silver question in a conversational way, although one of the longest of the documents, proved to be one of the most popular. A majority of these pamphlets dealt with the currency issue; but towards the end of the campaign, as the effect of the early hurrah for Bryan and free silver wore off, an increasing demand was made upon the Committee for protectionist reading matter. Something like 275 different pamphlets and leaflets were circulated, and they were printed in German, French, Spanish, Italian, Swedish, Norwegian, Danish, Dutch and Hebrew, as well as English.

The National Committee had this reading matter prepared, but it was usually shipped to the State Committees for actual distribution. To a constantly increasing extent, however, the documents were sent direct to individuals from Chicago. They found by experience that the State and County Committees frequently did not cooperate with sufficient energy or sufficient intelligence in the distribution of the reading matter. Two weeks before the election, so it is said, several carloads of pamphlets had not been unloaded from the freight cars at Columbus, Ohio. The Committee also distributed material direct to the newspapers. Country journals with an aggregate circulation of 1,650,000 received three and one-half columns of specially prepared matter every week. Another list of country newspapers with an aggregate weekly circulation of about 1,000,000 were furnished with plates, while to still another class were supplied ready prints. Of course cartoons, posters, inscriptions and buttons were manufactured by the carload — the most popular poster being the five-colored, single-sheet lithograph circulated as early as the St. Louis Convention, bearing a portrait of Mr. McKinley with the inscription underneath, "The Advance Agent of Prosperity."

The most serious problem confronting the Committee was that of raising the money necessary to pay the expenses of the campaign. Its work had been organized on a scale unprecedented in the political history of the country. The cost of its organization and of its bureaus of printed matter and speakers was substantially larger than that incurred during previous campaigns. It was not only conducting an unusually exhaustive and expensive educational canvass, but it was assuming a good deal of work usually undertaken and paid for by the State Committees. Unless a proportionately large amount of money could be raised, the operations of the National Committee must be curtailed and Mr. McKinley's chances of success compromised.

The task of raising this money belonged chiefly to Mr. Hanna. He had planned this tremendous campaign, and he must find the means of paying for it. Neither was it as obvious as it is now how this was to be done. The customary method of voluntary contribution, helped out by a little dunning of the protected manufacturers, was wholly insufficient. Money in sufficient volume could not be raised locally. The dominant issue endangered the national financial system, and the money must be collected in New York, the headquarters of national finance. In 1896 Mr. Hanna was not as well known in New York as he subsequently became. He was a Middle Western business man with incidental Eastern connections. Wall Street had not favored McKinley's nomination. Its idea of a presidential candidate had been Mr. Levi P. Morton. It required some persuasion and some enlightenment before it would unloosen its purse to the required extent.

Mr. James J. Hill states that on August 15, just when the strenuous work of the campaign was beginning, he met Mr. Hanna by accident in New York and found the chairman very much discouraged. Mr. Hanna described the kind of work which was planned by the Committee and its necessarily heavy expense. He had been trying to raise the needed money, but with only small success. The financiers of New York would not contribute. It looked as if he might have to curtail his plan of campaign, and he was so disheartened that he talked about quitting. Mr. Hill immediately offered to accompany Mr. Hanna on a tour through the high places of Wall Street, and during the next five days they succeeded in collecting as much money as was immediately necessary. Thereafter Mr. Hanna did not need any further personal introduction to the leading American financiers. Once they knew him, he gained their confidence. They could contribute money to his war chest, with none of the qualms which they suffered when "giving up" to a regular political "boss." They knew that the money would be honestly and efficiently expended in order to secure the victory of Republican candidates.

Never again during the campaign of 1896 or during any campaign managed by Mr. Hanna was the National Committee pinched for cash.

With the assistance of his newly established connections in the financial district, Mr. Hanna organized the business of collecting contributions as carefully as that of distributing reading matter. Inasmuch as the security of business and the credit system of the country were involved by the issues of the campaign, appeals were made to banks and business men, irrespective of party affiliations, to come to the assistance of the National Committee. Responsible men were appointed to act as local agents in all fruitful neighborhoods for the purpose both of soliciting and receiving contributions. In the case of the banks, a regular assessment was levied, calculated, I believe, at the rate of one-quarter of one per cent of their capital, and this assessment was for the most part paid. It is a matter of public record that large financial institutions such as the life insurance companies, were liberal contributors. The Standard Oil Company gave $250,000, but this particular corporation was controlled by men who knew Mr. Hanna and was unusually generous. Other corporations and many individual capitalists and bankers made substantial but smaller donations. Mr. Hanna always did his best to convert the practice from a matter of political begging on the one side and donating on the other into a matter of systematic assessment according to the means of the individual and institution.

Although the amount of money raised was, as I have said, very much larger than in any previous or in any subsequent campaign its total has been grossly exaggerated. It has been estimated as high as $12,000,000; but such figures have been quoted only by the yellow journals and irresponsible politicians. A favorite estimate has been $6,000,000 or $7,000,000; but even this figure is almost twice as large as the money actually raised. The audited accounts of the Committee exhibited collections of a little less than $3,500,000, and some of this was not spent. Of this sum a little over $3,000,000 came from New York and its vicinity, and the rest from Chicago and its vicinity. In 1892 the campaign fund had amounted to about $1,500,000, but the Committee had finished some hundreds of thousands of dollars in debt. The money raised in New York was spent chiefly in Chicago. To the $335,000 collected in the West $1,565,000 was added from the East, thus bringing the expenditures of the Chicago headquarters up to $1,970,000.

The way in which this money was spent affords a good idea of the scope of the Committee's work. The general office cost about $13,000 in the salaries of the staff and in miscellaneous expenses. The Bureau of Printed Matter spent approximately $472,000 in printing, and $32,000 in salaries and other expenses. The cost of the Bureau of Speakers was $140,000. The shipping department needed some $80,000. About $276,000 was contributed to the assistance of local and special organizations, and no less than $903,000 to the State Committees. These figures are official and confirm what has already been stated. The distribution of pamphlets, the furnishing of speakers and the expenses of organization account for half the expenses of the Chicago headquarters. The State Committees, on whom devolved the work of special canvassing and of getting out the vote, claimed the remainder. A large appropriation to the Congressional Committee was furnished from New York. Towards the end of the campaign money came pouring in so abundantly that the

Committee balanced its books with a handsome surplus. It was urged upon Mr. Hanna that out of this surplus he reimburse himself for his expenses in nominating McKinley, but, of course, he refused to consider the suggestion.

The question of political ethics involved by the collection of so much money from such doubtful sources, if it ever was a question, has been settled. American public opinion has emphatically declared that no matter what the emergency, it will not permit the expenses of elections to be met by individuals and corporations which may have some benefit to derive from the result. But in 1896 public opinion had not declared itself, and the campaign fund of that year was unprecedented only in its size. It resulted from the development of a practice of long standing, founded on a real need of money with which to pay election expenses, and shared wherever opportunity permitted by both political parties. Mr. Hanna merely systematized and developed a practice which was rooted deep in contemporary American political soil, and which was sanctioned both by custom and, as he believed, by necessity.

The unnecessary complications of the American electoral system, requiring as it does the transaction of an enormous amount of political business, resulted inevitably in the development of political professionalism and in large election expenses. In the beginning these expenses were paid chiefly by candidates for office or office-holders. When supplies from this source were diminished, while at the same time expenses were increasing, politicians naturally sought some other sources of income, and they found one of unexpected volume in the assessments which they could levy upon business men and corporations, which might be injured or benefited by legislative action. The worst form which the practice took consisted in the regular contribution by certain large corporations to the local machines of both parties for the purpose either of protection against legislative annoyance or for the purchase of favors. During the latter part of the eighties and the early nineties this practice of bipartisan contributions prevailed in all those states in which many corporations existed and in which the parties were evenly divided in strength.

We have seen that an essential and a useful part of Mark Hanna's political activity had been connected with the collection of election expenses for the Republican party in Cleveland and Ohio. Under prevailing conditions his combination of personal importance both in business and in politics was bound to result in some such connection. But he had never been associated with the least defensible phase of the practice — viz. that of contributing to both machines for exclusively business purposes. He was a Republican by conviction, and he spent his own money and collected money from others for the purpose of electing Republican candidates to office. As he became prominent in politics, however, it so happened that the business interests of the country came to rely more and more on the Republican party. It was the organization which supported the protective tariff which was more likely to control legislation in the wealthier states, and which finally declared in favor of the gold standard. The Republican party became the representative of the interests and needs of American business, and inevitably American business men came liberally to its support. Their liberality was increased because of the personal confidence of the business leaders in Mr. Hanna's efficiency and good faith, and because in 1896 these leaders, irrespective of partisan ties, knew that the free coinage of silver would be disastrous to the credit and prosperity of the country. In that year the Republicans happened to be entirely right and the Democrats entirely wrong upon a dominant economic issue. The economic inexperience and immaturity of large parts of the United States and the readiness of a section of the American people to follow untrustworthy leadership in economic matters, had given legitimate business an essential interest in the triumph of one of the political parties. Business men can scarcely be blamed for fighting the heresy in the only probably effective manner.

Mark Hanna's reputation has suffered because of his connection with this system, but closely associated as he was with it, he is not to be held responsible for its blameworthy aspects. All he did was to make it more effective by virtue of his able expenditure of the money, of his systematization of the collections, and by the confidence he inspired that the money would be well spent. The real responsibility is much more widely distributed. The system was the inevitable result of the political organization and ideas of the American democracy and the relation which had come to prevail between American political and economic life. As soon as it began to work in favor of only one of the two political parties it was bound to be condemned by public opinion; but the methods adopted to do away with it may be compared to an attempt to obliterate the pest of flies merely by the slaughter of the insects. The question of how necessarily heavy election expenses are to be paid, particularly in exciting and closely contested campaigns, has been hitherto evaded.

Mr. Hanna's opponents have, however, made him individually and in a sense culpably responsible for a traditional relation between politics and business. The economic issue dividing the parties in 1896 was easily perverted into a class issue, and the class issue was exploited for all it was worth by the other side. The vituperation which the representatives of the poor are privileged to pour out on the representatives of the well-to-do was concentrated on Mark Hanna. He became the victim of a series of personal attacks, which for their persistence, their falsity and their malignancy have rarely been equalled in the history of political invective. Mark Hanna was quoted and pictured to his fellow-countrymen as a sinister, corrupt type of the Money-man in politics — unscrupulous, inhumanly selfish, the sweater of his own employees, the relentless enemy of organized labor, the besotted plutocrat, the incarnate dollar-mark.

The peculiar malignancy of these attacks was due partly to certain undesirable innovations which had recently appeared in American journalism. Mr. William R. Hearst was beginning his career as a political yellow journalist. He was the first newspaper publisher to divine how much of an opportunity had been offered to sensational journalism by the increasing economic and political power of American wealth; and he divined also that the best way to use the opportunity would be to attach individual responsibility to the worst aspects of a system. The system must be concentrated in a few conspicuous individual examples, and they must be ferociously abused and persistently vilified. The campaign of 1896 offered a rare chance to put his discovery into practice, and inevitably Mr. McKinley and Mr. Hanna, as the most conspicuous Republican leaders, were selected as the best victims of assault.

The personal attack on Mark Hanna was begun somewhat before Mr. McKinley's nomination. Early in 1896 Alfred Henry Lewis had published in the New York Journal an article claiming to be an interview with Mr. Hanna and making him appear as a fool and a braggart. In a letter to the owner of the Journal, Mr. Hanna protested vigorously against the misrepresentation, but without effect. Later the personal attack upon him was reduced to a system. For a while Mr. Lewis appears to have been stationed in Cleveland in order to tell lies about him. He was depicted as a monster of sordid and ruthless selfishness, who fattened himself and other men on the flesh and blood of the common people. This picture of the man was stamped sharply on the popular consciousness by the powerful but brutal caricatures of Homer Davenport. Day after day he was portrayed with perverted ability and ingenuity as a Beast of Greed, until little by little a certain section of public opinion became infected by the poison. Journals of similar tendencies elsewhere in the country followed the lead with less ability and malignancy but with similar persistence.

When these attacks began Mr. Hanna was strongly tempted to bring suit for libel and to cause the arrest of Alfred Henry Lewis; but after consulting with his friends he decided that Lewis and Hearst were aiming at precisely this result — with the expectation of profiting more from the notoriety and the appearance of persecution than they would lose in damages. So he decided to disregard the attacks, libellous as they probably were, and he continued to do so until the end. But he was very much wounded by them and suffered severely from the vindictive and grotesque misrepresentation. Like all men whose disposition was buoyant and expansive, and whose interests were active and external, he was dependent upon the approval of his associates. As the scope of his political activity increased, the approbation which he wanted and needed had to come from a widely extended public opinion. Hence, while he was by no means a thin-skinned man, and was accustomed to stand up under the blows received in the rough and tumble of political fighting, he could not but wince under a personal distortion which was at once so gross and brutal, and yet so insidious and so impossible to combat. He had been brought up in the midst of the good-fellowship characteristic of the Middle West of the last generation. He was used to a social atmosphere of mutual confidence and a general and somewhat promiscuous companionship. He was accustomed to deal fairly with other men and to be dealt fairly with by them; and this concentration upon his own person of a class hatred and suspicion wounded and staggered him, until he became accustomed to it, and was better able to estimate its real effect upon public opinion.

The practice of attaching to a few conspicuous individuals a sort of criminal responsibility for widely diffused political and economic abuses and evils has, of course, persisted; and in so large a country as the United States it has necessarily been performed by newspapers and magazines. The people who have participated in this pleasant and profitable business are recommended to ponder the following sentence from Aristotle's "Politics," which is as true of the American Democracy as it was of that of Greece. "The gravest dangers to democracy," says Aristotle, usually occur "from the intemperate conduct of the demagogs, who force the propertied classes to combine by instituting malicious prosecutions against individuals or by inciting the masses against them as a body."

Whatever one may think about the rights and wrongs of the campaign fund of 1896, it must be admitted that it served its purpose. If the campaign of instruction had not been organized on the scale undertaken by the National Committee, the election of Mr. McKinley might never have taken place. The Committee itself had for a long time no confidence in the success of its labors. Not until early in October did they begin to feel that the tide had been turned. The decisiveness of the result must not deceive any one into the belief that it was inevitable. The momentum and enthusiasm attained toward the middle of October by the campaign on behalf of Mr. McKinley's election was the result of the vigorous, exhaustive and systematic work performed by the National Committee during the two previous months.

Mr. Hanna had a method of conducting a political campaign, not unlike that of a coach in training a foot-ball team. His attempt was gradually to wind up public opinion until it was charged with energy and confidence. The different moves in the campaign were planned in advance. All the general preparations were completed by a certain date. There followed some particularly vigorous special onslaughts on particular states; and when this work was satisfactorily accomplished, preparations were made to hold the ground while the hard work was concentrated on other less doubtful states. The execution of this general plan was carried out with the utmost care and vigor. The whole organization was inspired by the energy and confidence of its chief. Gradually a contagious enthusiasm and élan was communicated to the entire body. The different lines of work converged towards the end of the campaign. Their effect was cumulative, and their ultimate goal a condition of complete readiness on the Saturday night before election.

In the year 1896 Mr. Hanna was conducting his first National Campaign, and he was, perhaps, over-eager. At all events he pushed his preparations somewhat too hard. He was ready for the election a week before election day, and he feared that he could not hold his ground. He was afraid, that is, of overtraining; and the last week was a period for him of intense uneasiness. And he might well be uneasy, because the country had been worked up to a condition of high excitement. By skilful management and a good cause the hurrah for Bryan had been converted into a hurrah for McKinley. Enthusiasm could not be maintained at such a pitch, and if it began to subside, the recession might attain a dangerous volume. His fears proved to be unnecessary. The electorate had not only been worked up to a high state of enthusiasm, but they had been convinced. The victory on election day realized Mr. Hanna's highest hopes and expectations. No President since U. S. Grant entered office supported by so large a proportion of the American people as did William McKinley.

James A. Barnes:

MYTHS OF THE BRYAN CAMPAIGN

L AST year was the fiftieth anniversary of the great campaign of 1896. That would have been an opportune time for re-examining the significant events of the contest. But, preoccupied with the problems of existence, plagued by fitful wonderings as to where the "brave new world" had gone, and engulfed in a tide of students, historians took little note of the occasion. It would seem that a half century should have produced some carefully synthesized studies of the tremendous forces that were coming into conflict in the decade of the eighteen nineties. While there is a vast amount of printed material on the subject available in one form or another, no real story of the Bryan campaign has as yet appeared. A recent writer in compiling an extensive agrarian bibliography for the period commented that the best account still remains *The First Battle*. Though Bryan probably was, as he said, fully aware of the "magnitude of the issues involved," the volume, prepared in the year of the event, emphasizes too much the political mechanics and pays too little attention to the profound implications of the contest. Marian Silveus' "The Antecedents of the Bryan Campaign," an unpublished University of Wisconsin doctoral dissertation, is scarcely wider in scope, and the chapter heading frequently used in texts — "The Battle of the Standards" — reveals its own limitations.

It is possible in a brief paper only to indicate some of the basic factors in the campaign and to mention some of the misconceptions that have had their day and in many cases still survive. The real

James A. Barnes, "Myths of the Bryan Campaign," *Mississippi Valley Historical Review*, XXXIV, No. 3 (December, 1947), 367–369, 380–383, 394–404. Used by permission.

significance of the Bryan campaign cannot be found in the answers, however important, to the two questions: first, Did Bryan win the nomination by his great oration? and, second, Would sixteen to one have, as Dean Neil Carothers said in the *Dictionary of American History,* brought suicide to the nation? The year 1896 was a momentous year not because of great happenings but because of great implications. It came in a period when old philosophies were dying and new ones, some of which are not even yet out of their swaddling clothes, were struggling to be born. It came when the farmer was being forever pushed away from the few remaining men who processed the products of his toil; the blacksmith who made his wagon and the miller who ground his grain were falling before the same industrial giants who were making of agriculture a secondary occupation. It came when the laborer was being irrevocably separated from his employer and made merely a cog in a vast machine that was kept on its pace by foremen, often bigots in their own little worlds. It came when the city was rising to supremacy. It came too, this year 1896, when industrial and financial concentration had reached tremendous heights. Ownership and management were divorced, and each year fewer plants turned out ever-increasing amounts of goods. Privilege was everywhere apparent, and trusts, including a money trust (so said the congressmen later), dominated the nation.

The very success of industry made the campaign of 1896 a notable one. The basic railroad system was nearing completion, and the over-all physical structure of the nation was far advanced. America had passed that phase in the development of a going concern when the means of survival and growth — regardless of personal or institutional trage-

dies — are paramount. The country had reached that point where progress no longer hinged upon heedless disregard of all except general principles and policies, but began to revolve around the concept that human beings are the most important components of human governments and other human institutions, industrial and otherwise. Thus it is that the twentieth century has materially been primarily concerned with consumer goods and politically been interested in the welfare of individuals — with all the conflict and controversy that that implies.

The rising consciousness of responsibility for the people of the nation brought also a change from a negative to a positive philosophy of governmental action. The speeches and other utterances of national statesmen before the middle nineties are filled to overflowing with earnest warnings that alleviating laws or even public discussion of the problems of human welfare and human impositions — freely admitted — would bring first and foremost penalties to those unable to protect themselves. Such action, it was argued, would only make the poor prey to the privileged. Nowhere in national thinking was there a conception of direct control of the greedy who might take advantage of efforts at reform. In no field were the people more urged to bear their ills uncomplainingly lest greater troubles come than in that of finance.

These things, garnished with poverty, drought, grasshoppers, high freight charges, and other miseries and impositions, are the blood and the bone of the campaign of 1896. Harvey Wish in his article on "John Peter Altgeld and the Background of the Campaign of 1896" cautions his readers that to tie the campaign to silver alone is to overlook the social and economic factors. One might add that it is to miss the essence of the campaign as well. To speak of the silver crusade without envisioning its economic and social aspects as its major components is not merely to leave Hamlet out of the play; it is to omit the play altogether. Silver was but a symbol of things deep and fundamental, and its wisdom can be denied without lessening the significance of the revolt that Bryan led. The "Great Commoner" saw faintly at least what Woodrow Wilson seventeen years later put into academic words and what Franklin D. Roosevelt thirty-seven years afterwards turned into the language of the people. . . .

Many of the statements concerning Bryan as a possible nominee of the party are open to question. *He was not an unknown.* It was noted in Albert Shaw's *Review of Reviews* in August, 1896, that it was the fashion of some eastern newspapers and not a few prominent personages to sneer at the Nebraskan's candidacy and to profess never to have heard of him before his speech at Chicago. "If, indeed," said the writer, "they had not heard of Mr. Bryan before, they had failed to follow closely the course of American politics in the past eight years. As a Democratic member of the Ways and Means Committee through two Congresses, Mr. Bryan was by all odds the ablest and strongest orator on the Democratic side of the House. His subsequent canvass for the United States senatorship in Nebraska was noteworthy and conspicuous on many accounts." Several years later Josephus Daniels observed:

Writers of that day and later historians have said that an unknown man captured the convention by one speech. Not so. Bryan did not suddenly reach that pinnacle. Behind that memorable hour was a brilliant record of achievement in the halls of Congress and on the hustings. He had won two elections to the National House in rock-ribbed Republican districts in Nebraska. He had charmed "listening Senates" in a noble argument for tariff reform which Champ Clark declared was "the greatest and most brilliant Bryan ever delivered." In the battle between giants in the epoch of silver discussions the pebble in the sling of the young David from Nebraska had compassed the political death of more than one political Goliath

Certainly Bryan's speeches on the tariff and on the repeal of the Sherman silver law had been widely circulated. Moreover, Bryan had probably talked to more voters throughout the farming regions than had any other individual at the convention. *That no delegates were pledged to present and support his name was of no significance.* He could have had many sponsors, but admitted followers would have meant admitted opponents and would have made his Chicago appeal seem to be directed only to those who were not yet under his banner rather than to the whole people who were demanding relief. He had been thought of as a candidate long before 1896. The repeal fight of 1893 had made it reasonably certain that the majority of the Democratic party would in 1896 seek a Westerner or a Southerner to be its leader if it could muster the power to overthrow the Cleveland forces. In both the West and the South there was a widespread feeling that the time had come when the voters must demand their "just dues." Bryan's defeat in the Nebraska senatorial race in 1894 furthered his cause, and his speeches over the agrarian states brought many advocates. A Louisiana newspaper commented in mid-1895: "Mr. Bryan, though but 35 years of age, has made a reputation that any man might justly envy. He is considered one of the greatest orators of the century; a man honest of purpose and convictions. With this reputation he came to New Orleans, and there he made a 'hit' that has increased his strength and popularity to such an extent that it is whispered he will be the Democratic nominee for president on a free-silver platform." By April, 1896, many individuals were quietly working for Bryan's nomination. Circulars were being distributed in Illinois, and admirers in Nebraska, North Carolina, Mississippi, Louisiana, Texas, Arkansas, and other states were urging his selection among their friends. It was not in any concerted or open action, however, that Bryan had his strength; it was in the friendly predisposition of the mass of the delegates that he had hopes. Too much emphasis has in some cases been given Governor Altgeld's so-called brutal chastisement in wiring Bryan on June 12, "Find everywhere great admiration for you but an almost unanimous sentiment that you are not available for president this time." The sentiment came largely from leaders who themselves were tempting the lightning. That fact is evidenced by the statement, "All feel you should be in new cabinet if we succeed," for the men who would actually choose the nominee by their votes were not interested in cabinets. *It was not important that Bryan was not a delegate at the opening of the convention.* Since the silver forces were in overwhelming majority, the seating of the contesting Nebraska delegation of which Bryan was the head was merely a matter of form. Once it was seated, it was equally certain that the most effective orator of the party would make a speech. It would have been stupid to enter debate with the gold men without using the outstanding asset at hand.

No accident was involved in the nomination. The convention knew what it wanted, and Bryan knew what the convention wanted; moreover, he had more than a suspicion that he alone possessed whatever that was. Circumstances were

such that one thing followed the other logically. Bryan was careful to see that nothing interfered with the course of events. He refused even after the convention met, says Josephus Daniels, to let the North Carolina delegation announce its support. The oration was but his last step, and that step was made certain when the silverites defeated the followers of gold. It would be foolish to disparage the force of Bryan's words. The speech was of tremendous importance, but the things that gave it its effect were already in existence before it was delivered. If the "Boy Orator" won anything singlehanded with his own jawbone, it was the nominations of the Populist and Silver parties. The selection of Bryan did not unseat Cleveland; it only marked the end of dual leadership in a new group that had firmly pitched its tents on Democratic grounds. So far as the party was concerned, Cleveland had been dead for three years and safely buried for three days, and there was not power in all the land ever to roll away the stone that closed his sepulcher.

Third,* *that Bryan toured the country a firebrand, a knight of gold.* It is true that the Democratic candidate of 1896 did travel thousands of miles and make hundreds of speeches. That as a departure in American politics was interesting. It was not important as a part of the campaign. The fact that the decision in the contest would be made by that small group of states lying roughly in the Y the two forks of which are the Ohio and the Mississippi was recognized long before the silver Democrats gained control of the party. There Bryan delivered by far the largest number of speeches; there silver and gold came cheek by jowl; there agriculture and industry challenged each other — and there Bryan lost the campaign. He made

* The preceding two points have been omitted. Ed.

forage raids into the outposts such as Kentucky, Tennessee, West Virginia, Missouri, Nebraska, and North and South Dakota and fought hard for Iowa. The eastern journeys were incidental to the immediate point in view.

Fourth, *that the issue was between honest money and dishonest money.* The issue of 1896, while it was tied to free coinage, was infinitely wider than a narrow definition of a dollar. The honest dollar is difficult to identify. It is one thing to the debtor, another to the creditor, and yet another to the financial philosopher. The silver followers of the last quarter of the nineteenth century referred to such a dollar as "the dollar of the contract"; to them it was a social instrument that took from man no more toil at one time than at another. The gold men, on the other hand, saw it as a dollar that regardless of any official markings of a state would because of its intrinsic value be the same anywhere in the world; to them it was an instrument (created by nature and directed by natural laws) for use in buying and selling, for it would pay debts, international as well as national, though they surely did not believe it would purchase in all markets however distant the same number of pigs and calves and loaves of bread. In the nineteen thirties Franklin D. Roosevelt described the honest dollar as one that would not change in value from year to year. A short time later one of the "elder statesmen" declared from a park bench that it was a dollar that unearthed centuries hence from the grave of any of us would still buy a haircut or pay for pressing a pair of pants. Fundamentally, then, the conflict is still the same, notwithstanding the fact that our laws and our policies have followed the demands of the Greenbackers, the Populists, and the new Democrats that Bryan led. Without attempting to

answer the question of what the honest dollar was or is, one can safely say that in 1896 the Americans who called silver — that is, the money that silver then represented to the people — the honest dollar were far more numerous than those who so referred to gold.

Fifth, *that new sources of gold and other factors brought prosperity and changed the election by stripping Bryan of agrarian votes. . . .*

Sixth, *that the Bryan campaign was a "crackpot circus."* A host of fundamental issues were pressing for consideration in 1896. These issues have continued to be fundamental; indeed, they have made up the real substance of our twentieth-century domestic political controversies. One may if he wishes say that sixteen to one as the talisman to which farm people tied their hopes was idiotic, but he cannot fail to see in Bryan's speech and in the Democratic platform the foundations of many things that soon became paramount in the nation, whether sponsored by the insurgents, the progressives, the Wilson forces, or the legions of Franklin D. Roosevelt. The things have come, however, not as agrarian but as urban issues. Within a few years the depiction of poverty and privilege was to swell the subscription rolls of a number of metropolitan magazines to unbelievable size; in less than a decade corporations were called on with at least some sincerity to answer to the people; and within less than two decades there was open admission that a money trust existed, there was an income tax, and, whether banking went out of the business of government or not, there was no doubt that there was government in banking.

The campaign of 1896, so far as the candidates and the leading political speakers were concerned, was cast on a high plane. Bryan and McKinley and Carlisle and others talked with earnestness and with comprehension of the fact that America stood at some sort of crossroad. If the conflict revealed aspects of a "crackpot circus," it was the woefully ignorant and the fearfully intellectual who were mostly responsible. Few times have our leading journals demonstrated so flagrantly closed minds and blatant propensities. The *Nation* and the *Commercial and Financial Chronicle* perhaps led all the rest. Some of the newspapers outdid even them. The description of the convention by the Philadelphia *Press* on July 10 will serve admirably as an illustration:

The Jacobins are in full control at Chicago. No large political movement in America has ever before spawned such hideous and repulsive vipers. The Vallandighams of the war period were odious, but even they did not belong to this serpent brood. The Altgelds and Tillmans who have thrust aside the old leaders of the Democracy and have seized the reins of control incarnate a spirit of Communism and Anarchy which is new to American politics on any large scale. . . .

This riotous platform is the concrete creed of the mob. It is rank Populism intensified and edged with hate and venom. It rests upon the four corner stones of organized Repudiation, deliberate Confiscation, chartered Communism, and enthroned Anarchy. Such a noxious and nefarious profession of faith has never before been made in this country even by an escaped band of lunatics. It begins with falsehood, advances through war upon the social fabric and ends with the unleashing of the mob. Its demand for the reign of the fifty cent dollar is only the first step. It betrays the real scheme when it proposes to destroy all national bank currency, and give the Government power to issue unlimited fiat paper money. A billion would fail, and the printing press would be made to turn out two billions! Then we should have dollars not of fifty cents, but of forty cents, twenty cents, nothing! . . . .

The platform in every vital part appeals to everything that is low and debased and vicious in human nature. In its moral quality and in its public policy it bespeaks the most lawless, irresponsible, incendiary group of besotted leaders who have ever been thrown to the surface even in the worst paroxysms of American demagogism.

Not satisfied, the paper returned to the same theme the next day to say among other things:

The speech of Mr. Bryan which brought him to the front was a specious but shallow display of rhetorical buncombe. . . . The unkempt mob of agitators saw in it a glittering embodiment of their crude and disordered ideas, and they made the exponent of their creed of nihilism the hero of their crusade of destruction.

Only the *Review of Reviews* among the publications examined took a dignified and scholarly attitude throughout the campaign. The editor wrote in August:

The men who carried the Chicago platform were doubtless affected by such a wave of emotional excitement as sometimes sways great religious gatherings, but they were not lunatics or revolutionists. They were self-respecting American citizens, who detest anarchy, abhor repudiation, and occupy their present attitude with the clearest consciences and strongest convictions that have swayed their political action at any time for many years. Let the facts be fairly faced and told. The moral superiority in the convention did not lie with the masterful politicians of the Hill and Whitney type, who went to Chicago with the impression that they might through long experience in convention management divide the ranks of the free-silver majority and secure a compromise result. Against the earnestness, openness, and almost fanatical intensity of the free-silver majority, the calculating politicians were simply helpless. . . . it does not follow for a moment that we consider enthusiasm to be a safe guide in the field of monetary science.

Notwithstanding the facts that emotions were deeply stirred on both sides, that Godkin and other critics condemned every farmer who protested against his condition as a worthless, suspicious, and indolent character who sat "idly waiting for the demagogue and the craze-monger," and that the charge was often repeated that ignorant men "were shaking the pennies in their pockets and gleefully looking forward to free silver, when, they believed, the pennies would by some magic become dollars," the campaign was a thoughtful one. Before it had ended, practically everyone in the nation had become involved in the discussion. "There have been in Michigan comparatively few speeches from noted men," said Professor Henry C. Adams of the University of Michigan, "but meetings are held in hundreds of schoolhouses nightly. Posters are used, and they aim to be arguments rather than caricatures. The campaign is earnest, and for the most part courteous. It is a campaign of discussion and education." The unlettered as well as the lettered, government clerks as well as national statesmen, and the poor as well as the rich entered into the argument. Professor J. Laurence Laughlin bemoaned the fact that the uneducated, "capable of holding but one idea at a time," had been misled to follow silver by "the wiliest managers" who ever entered American politics. Professor Frank W. Taussig and Professor Edward A. Ross were doubtful that gold was an unmixed blessing, and Professor Richard T. Ely felt that free silver was a divergence from the real road of reform that might delay sound development and social progress for many years. Some understood the widespread social

and economic questions involved, while others saw only the simple question of good money versus bad money. Henry Cabot Lodge when the election was over was thankful that the old, the rich, and the educated had defeated the dishonest and the revolutionary. E. W. Codington declared in the *Forum* that it would "not be easy for the student of the future to repress a smile when he reads the history of the nineteenth century and discovers that learned men seriously discussed the question, 'How much money *per capita* ought to be in circulation among the people?'" "It is certain," he went on, "that only the antiquary of the future will find any meaning in the phrase quoted. Assuming that some grave professor shall be able to explain it all, will not that same student wonder why a people, ingenious enough to augment a short supply of money by substituting therefor more evidences of debt, and to curtail a long supply by refusing to coin one of its money metals, was not able to increase its crop of sugar or decrease an excessive crop of cotton by the same factitious methods?" And, as though to make it certain that the campaign would always be known as a "crackpot circus," Secretary of Agriculture J. Sterling Morton wrote on November 16 in his annual report:

The constant complaint by the alleged friends of the farmers, and by some farmers themselves, is that the Government does nothing for agriculture. In conventions and congresses it has been proclaimed that the farmers of the country are almost universally in debt, despondent, and suffering. Largely these declarations are without foundation. Their utterance is a belittlement of agriculture and an indignity to every intelligent and practical farmer of the United States. The free and independent farmers of this country are not impoverished; they are not mendicants; they are not wards of the

Government to be treated to annuities, like Indians upon a reservation. On the other hand, they are the representatives of the oldest, most honorable, and most essential occupation of the human race. Upon it all other vocations depend for subsistence and prosperity. The farmer is the co-partner of the elements. His intelligently directed efforts are in unison with the light and heat of the sun, and the success of his labors represents the commingling of the raindrops and his own sweat.

Legislation can neither plow nor plant. The intelligent, practical, and successful farmer needs no aid from the Government. The ignorant, impractical, and indolent farmer deserves none. . . . It is a beneficent arrangement of the order of things and the conditions of human life that legislators are not permitted to repeal, amend, or revise the laws of production and distribution.

Whatever its label, the campaign of 1896 must take its place as one of the most significant in American political history. That is true not only because of the matters openly discussed but also because of the basic underlying issues, and these issues ran deeper than the mere fact that there had been poor crops for several years. The contest made of the nation a public forum at a time when some of the questions had only barely come to the surface. The decision, however, was rendered on a much narrower basis than the wide sweep of the principles set forth in whole or in part in the Democratic platform. Bryan was defeated by that fear of something we know not of, for the bare bodkin of free silver on the tongues of the gold advocates conjured up evils more formidable even than those that existed. He was defeated by a flood of propaganda, and he was defeated by coercion. The coercion was obvious. Men *were* fired, men *were* told that free silver meant the end of their jobs, men *were* refused employment because of their monetary

sentiments, and men with mortgages *were* asked how they would vote. Industrial concerns, interested in their own welfare and the welfare of their workers as they saw the situation, brought immense pressure to bear upon their employees. Selfishness and greed were not necessarily involved. Cyrus H. McCormick, for instance, knew that only economic losses to himself could result when he wrote a Nebraska paper before the Bryan nomination:

The welfare of our country is to me of higher interest than any personal temporary gains. I am unalterably opposed to the free coinage of silver by the United States. . . . If national candidates should be elected upon that basis, I believe it would be the greatest misfortune that has overtaken our government in many years. I have been and am still a Democrat, but I cannot follow any party in the adoption of a measure which I firmly believe to be disastrous to the highest interests of the Nation. Therefore, I should vote for McKinley in preference to a free coinage silver Democrat.

McCormick, like other industrialists, took an active part in the campaign. His company sent every employee in the field a card on which he was asked to record his political sentiments and his opinion as to the situation in his territory. The corporation by its questionnaire method and its correspondence with the supervisory force sought only "reliable information in advance" that production might be wisely planned. Nevertheless, the consequence was political pressure, whether intentional or not. On August 24 E. F. Poore, collecting agent, wrote from Fort Wayne, Indiana:

With the exception of one of my men, we are all sound money. Mr. Giddings always having been a Democrat, and until yesterday I was fearful that he would vote the Silver ticket, but I had a long talk with him and I tried to picture the present election as purely a financial one, — party principles not being taken into consideration, — I tried to show to him that he must make it a personal matter and asked him if he could afford to jeopardize his future by voting dead against the interests of the Company who employed him and from whom he has drawn his bread and butter for a few years back. He had not looked at it that way and it opened up a new line of thought and I feel safe in guaranteeing that I can influence him to cast his vote for sound money the coming election. I shall labor with him from time to time, between now and then, and shall see that he casts it that way if he votes at all.

Everywhere the industrialists fought vigorously to preserve the existing standard of value; some, however, resented the criticisms that resulted from their efforts. Arthur E. Stilwell of Kansas City declared:

A lot of fellows who never had any business experience, and who couldn't make a living in any business vocation, insist upon the sole right to teaching finance to the people. When a man who makes finance a business chips in, they say he is a coercer of labor. Just because I employ 6000 men I have no right to tell those men, when they ask me, what I think about the questions before the country. The mission of financial enlightenment, these fellows maintain, belongs everlastingly to them. . . . Men of the sort that indulge in violent denunciations of me as a wolf in sheep's clothing may be honest, but very suspicious. . . . They are suspicious of everything about which they don't know anything, and, being utterly unable to comprehend the grave reason for my efforts to save the enterprise which employs our men, they swell up with suspicion.

But whatever their effect, limitless propaganda and widespread coercion were not wholly dominant factors in the gold victory. The forces that created the campaign also made it difficult if not impossible for Bryan to win. The city that had been growing almost unnoticed while eager throngs poured into the West had made of the agrarian before the West was filled the "hick" and the "hayseed," had appreciably reduced the ratio of the electoral vote of the agricultural states, and had tied to its own politics the workmen in its factories. Bryan, leading the last great agrarian army, lost every important urban center and the adjoining rural regions as well. He in part defeated himself by permitting the gold men to draw him on to their own battlefield and slay him with a single sword. A brilliant offensive that had begun on a wide field in July with the cry "We defy them" had by November turned into a defense on a narrow money front. There was sense in Mark Hanna's comment, "He's talking Silver all the time, and that's where we've got him," for the army that had girded itself in midsummer could not be held together on the single question of the standard of value.

The campaign of 1896 has run a devious course in the histories of the nation. Many accounts are too much concerned with the mechanics of the campaign, and they are too much burdened with the Bryan oration and the emotional upheaval that was an element of the contest. They reveal little about conditions of long standing and still less about the new forces that were pressing upward — though they may not have been fully understood by the people at the time. The readers often hear only a glorious voice that performed a miracle and a fanatical cry for sixteen to one that rose from the West. Economists and financiers too skirt the fundamental issues in an overwhelming desire to demonstrate the unwisdom of silver. Some writers have used the convention of 1896 to illustrate democracy at work, and others have glamorized the poverty of the farmers that they might excuse their ignorance, but few have intimated that real comprehension of the deep problems that were facing the new nation was lacking even in high places. Much that was said of money in that year 1896 was inexcusable. A few statesmen in administrative positions understood that something was wrong, but they saw in gold the same inevitableness that was eventually to return them to the dust from which they came. The men who in a few brief years took over the conduct of government, whether they realized it or not, struck their reform roots deep into the well-tilled soil of 1896. One wonders if Theodore Roosevelt's hostility to Bryan was in part based on the suspicion that some of his clothing, as suggested by the cartoonists, actually was borrowed. One wonders if Woodrow Wilson when he wrote for his inaugural in 1913,

We have been proud of our industrial achievements, but we have not hitherto stopped thoughtfully enough to count the human cost, the cost of lives snuffed out, of energies overtaxed and broken, the fearful physical and spiritual cost to the men and women and children upon whom the dead weight and burden of it all has fallen pitilessly the years through. The groans and agony of it all had not yet reached our ears, the solemn, moving undertone of our life, coming up out of the mines and factories and out of every home where the struggle had its intimate and familiar seat,

heard that moving undertone in its infancy, garbed in silver though it may have been, coming up out of the farms and the shops in another day. Did he think of an oration that in his *History of the American People* he had called "radical" when in recommending currency legislation he spoke of "mimic mastery" within the shelter of government and declared that "the control of the system of banking and of issue which our new laws are to set up must be public, not private, must be vested in the Government itself, so that the banks may be the instruments, not the masters, of business and of individual enterprise and initiative"? One wonders if Franklin D. Roosevelt ever reflected, as balloting reports came in, that Bryan had not been able to tap the swelling reservoir of urban poor. Though he probably did not, he could have read in the Cross of Gold speech: "There are those who believe that, if you will only legislate to make the well-to-do prosperous, their prosperity will leak through on those below. The Democratic idea, however, has been that if you legislate to make the masses prosperous, their prosperity will find its way up through every class which rests upon them." Regardless of the significance or insignificance of the restless stirrings of the eighties and nineties in the history of the twentieth century, it is obvious that America's interpreters greatly misinterpreted the protest, whatever its evils, of mature agrarianism in 1896 when urbanism was pushing up through it. The nation may be committing the same grave error in its interpretation of the protest, whatever its sins, of mature urbanism today when internationalism is pushing upward through it. There may be — as there was in 1896 — an obligation to find a better solution than some of the protesters are offering.

Charles E. Merriam: WILLIAM JENNINGS BRYAN

WILLIAM JENNINGS BRYAN is a different type of leader from any of those thus far considered. Here was a man who maintained himself in a position of very great political power for a generation, without a political organization, without wealth except his own earnings, without professional position, without holding office except for a brief period. Four years in Congress as a young man and two years as Secretary of State in his maturity constitute his official career. Yet his personal influence upon legislation and public policy is written large in American public life for over thirty years. Since 1892 he was defeated in all elections in which he appeared as a candidate, but no one during this time on the whole wielded greater influence over the minds of men politically than he did. Other men have been far more powerful at given moments than Bryan, but none maintained his ascendancy over the minds of millions of voters for so sustained a period as the Nebraska statesman. Both Roosevelt and Wilson were antedated and outlived by Bryan.

What are the secrets of the power of this notable figure in American political life? How did he maintain himself during all these years against the bitter opposition of many organization workers, against the pressure of the dominant industrial interests, in the face of newspaper attacks, and despite the criticism of the intellectuals? The analysis of this problem is one of the interesting studies in American politics.

Bryan's early life made him familiar with the farming conditions of central Illinois, with the urban situation in Chicago while a student of law, and later with the agrarian problem in Nebraska and the West. He was essentially the product of the economic and political conditions of the Middle West in the early '90s. His background was that of revolt, Western revolt, not so much against the political bosses and the spoils system as against industrial oligarchy, against railroads and trusts as instruments of attack upon agrarian prosperity and upon democracy. Agricultural distress and the fear of plutocracy are the bases of his attitude and career. Business depression fell heavily upon the farmer in the '90s, and made him ready for almost any measures of relief that offered promise of aid. The specific formula relied upon at that time was bimetalism or free silver which appealed to the farmer as likely to aid him in regaining his lost prosperity.

Bryan represented the West and the South as against the East and the Center of the country, and voiced their demand for drastic measures to help the agrarian, debtor communities. This was the same geographical group (relatively) that had elected Jefferson and Jackson and later supported Wilson. It did not bring victory to Bryan, but it brought steady support to his doctrines. Fundamentally it was not the currency or the tariff or imperialism that Bryan assailed, although he attacked all three of these at various times, but the tendency inherent in the current conditions to establish a plutocratic government. While he shifted the

From Charles E. Merriam, *Four American Party Leaders*. Copyright 1926 by The Macmillan Company and used with their permission.

specific issues of his campaigns from time to time, undoubtedly he faced in the same direction all of the time.

Throughout life Bryan was gifted with tremendous physical vitality. In college he was an "athlete" although not professionally trained or particularly gifted except in the standing broad jump. Yet he was never in any sense a sportsman, and was little interested in field sports or in fishing or hunting. Nevertheless he maintained a very high degree of physical fitness. He displayed unrivalled capacity for the stress and strain of political campaigns, and for political contacts of all sorts. His remarkable campaign of 1896 eclipsed all previous records in number of speeches and in persons reached. This untiring energy was evident throughout a generation of strenuous endeavor which would have torn most men to tatters, but which left the Nebraskan undisturbed and unruffled. In a country as large as the United States, his sheer strength and endurance were unquestionably significant factors in his political fortunes.

Bryan's intellectual interest from his early days in college was centered in oratory and debate. In both of these fields he soon learned to excel, early attained renown as an orator and a debater, and was made valedictorian of his class. His intellectual interests and capacities inclined him toward forensic struggles in which his readiness and aptness were difficult to match. His debates in Congress on the tariff and the income tax in the early '90s illustrate very well the peculiar facility with which his mind worked in parliamentary situations. As a controversialist, he was at all times a formidable foe, not to be despised by any of his countrymen. At any time a swift thrust might suddenly discomfit an opponent before he could realize what had happened. Not at all a close or profound

reasoner, he was nevertheless ready and acute, and disconcerting both in his ability to seize upon a weak spot of the opposition, and in the humorous twist with which his attack might be made. Given the arena of public conflict with the stage set for the contest and he was one of the most dangerous antagonists of his time.

Bryan was endowed with an equable temperament that left him calm and placid through many trying situations that would have unnerved less firmly balanced men. Had there been a test for stability and placidity of temperament, he would doubtless have ranked high. His great good humor and sweetness of disposition in the face of repeated defeat and rebuff under incessantly galling criticism was remarkable. It was said of Bryan at one time that his smile was so broad that he could whisper in his own ear. However that may have been, he remained serene in the face of assaults that would have crushed many another man.

The New York *Tribune* said of him, after the election of 1896:

The wretched, rattle-pated boy, posing in vapid vanity and mouthing resounding rottenness was not the real leader of that league of hell. He was only a puppet in the blood-imbued hands of Altgeld, the anarchist, and Debs, the revolutionist, and other desperadoes of that stripe. But he was a willing puppet, Bryan was, willing and eager. Not one of his masters was more apt than he at lies and forgeries and blasphemies, and all the nameless iniquities of that campaign against the Ten Commandments. He goes down with the cause and must abide with it in the history of infamy. He had less provocation than Benedict Arnold, less intellectual force than Aaron Burr, less manliness and courage than Jefferson Davis. He was the rival of them all in deliberate wickedness and treason to the Republic. His name belongs with theirs, neither the most brilliant, nor the most hateful in the list. Good riddance to it all: — To the conspiracy, the conspirators, and to the foul menaces of repudiation and anarchy against the life of the Republic.

But Mr. Bryan said:

I shall always carry with me grateful as well as pleasant recollections of newspaper men with whom I was thrown. They were a gentlemanly and genial crowd!

Bryan felt the current of popular movements with great sensitiveness. By way of illustration, he understood the force of agrarian discontent, of opposition to the policy of imperialism, of the widespread fear of plutocracy. Later he sensed the dry movement. He interpreted the general desire for peace, and reflected it in his wide movement for the negotiation of peace treaties. He undertook the championship of government ownership of railroads, but abandoned it after he discovered the stout elements of opposition. It may be said that he was not always successful in finding the main positive current of national sentiment, but at any rate he found a strong current whether the main one or not. He did not succeed in interpreting Eastern sentiment as well as Western, but his advocacy of anti-imperialism and of the peace movement was representative of other than Western sentiments. In general it may be said that he was more successful in the divination of the tendencies regarding moralistic movements than in dealing with economic movements or tendencies. But taking the period of a generation during which he was called upon to interpret the social political forces, he was certainly uncommonly sensitive to the powerful tendencies of his day.

Bryan was likewise notable for his ability to see ways out of a given situation that puzzled the community. He was by no means always successful in hitting

upon plans that were adopted by the dominant forces in the state, but any rate he was fertile in expedients that were widely accepted, even if not given the force of law. He was an early champion of the income tax, which was not of course his own invention. He championed free silver as a panacea for the industrial and especially the agrarian evils of his day. He opposed the annexation of the Philippine Islands, and probably did not regret his course. He advocated the guaranty of bank deposits as a protection to the depositors. He contended for the dissolution of corporations in which one half of the total product consumed was controlled. He fought for the limitation of the use of the injunction in industrial disputes. He advocated the election of federal judges, "people's rule" in various forms, and the dry law. Some of these plans were adopted from campaigns well started and others were more nearly his own contrivance.

It will not of course be required of a leader that he shall be entitled to a patent on his political invention, but it may suffice if he becomes one of the chief champions of the idea. In this sense Bryan utilized many inventions, and in this sense he may be said to have possessed an inventive mind. He had more than the ordinary bent for the development of some remedy or way out of a distressing political situation. Perhaps the most notably original and successful of these was his plan for the general adoption of arbitration treaties, rudely interrupted by the outbreak of the Great War, but the principle of which went marching on. Broadly speaking Bryan was more of an evangelist than a constructor of original political plans or policies. Yet he undoubtedly had a certain flair for the contrivance of political plans, as ways of escape from certain distressing political situations.

Bryan was a group champion rather than a reconciler of divergent interests of conflicting views and tendencies. He stood for the cause of labor and of the under middle class, especially the agrarian group. He could find no common ground with business enterprises of the larger type and was constantly coming into conflict with their views and policies. He was rarely able to make an all-class combination of the type so frequently perfected by Roosevelt. He held the confidence of the South and West as geographical sections, but with many losses even here. He was frankly the spokesman for the groups that were out of the center of control and were striving to make themselves more effective in the national economic and political life.

Nor did Bryan deal successfully with the party organization which was frequently against him. This was not because he was vehement in his attacks upon the patronage system, for he at one time opposed the merit system, and was usually amenable to organization reason with respect to appointments. Bryan had of course great numbers of friends in the party organization and the numerous battles fought in his behalf could not leave his comrades untouched by a certain admiration for him. The larger bosses of the East and Center were, however, unreconciled to him, and used every occasion to discredit and thwart him. This attitude was not the result of disagreements actual or anticipated regarding the spoils of office, but because of the Bryan attacks upon corporate interests, and his identification of certain bosses with these big business interests. He was indeed in an awkward position, for if he defied Tammany his prospects for carrying a state like New York were somewhat diminished, while if on the other hand he made common cause with the Wigwam and greeted the chief cordially he was at once portrayed through the country as the friend and comrade of a pirate gang.

The Nebraska statesman maintained cordial relations with the religious groups, more extensively and successfully than any of his national contemporaries in politics. His religio-political speeches were widely heard and widely read, as for example, his *Prince of Peace,* and he found it easy to step from the arena of political debate to the calmer atmosphere of the church and the pulpit. There can be little doubt that much of the tenacious strength of Bryan came from the fact that he enjoyed a wide reputation as a "good" man, and from his unceasing and cordial contact with the leaders of the religious world as well as with the rank and file of the church congregations especially upon the Protestant side. In the heat of bitterly fought campaigns, Bryan might be vigorously and intemperately assailed, but between times he was the advocate of peace and of piety; the adroit and sincere defender of the interests of the church. He was orthodox in religion between his unorthodox political campaigns.

Thus his strength was peculiarly recruited from the agrarian group, the labor group, and the religious group cutting across economic class lines. He had developed here an unusual combination of elements of support, including both the highly pietistic rural group, and the more irreverent working class group of the cities. The labor group was not primarily interested in his moralistic measures but listened with deep interest when he assailed the abuse of the injunction in industrial disputes. The agricultural group was not concerned about the injunction, but were agog when he attacked the railroads and Wall Street and were impressed with his fundamental sincerity and piety. . . .

The outstanding qualities of Bryan

were his marvelous power of expression, his warmth of human contacts, his perception of great currents of community feeling, his undaunted courage and persistence, his deep religious fervor. In group diplomacy and in constructive measures, he was less notable. He was neither a demagogue, nor a great constructive statesman, but he was the greatest political evangelist of his day, — a prophet whose voice was raised again and again against the abuses of the time in which he lived. He saw the real danger of the establishment of plutocracy in free America, and the need of effective and continued protest, but he did not see so clearly the lines of advance or the methods of organizing effectively in law and administration the people's will. Roosevelt and Wilson entered into the land which Bryan had seen and toward which he had led the people for many years. Many estimates of Bryan have been made and doubtless they have been well made from special, particular points of view. But it seems to me that they have not fully grasped the significance of this character as a political leader. His democratic sympathies, his magical power of oratory, his persistence and courage, his sweetness of temper, his deep religio-political fervor; — these endeared him to great masses of people, who would not have been attracted by an efficient administrator or a constructive political inventor. Whether he thought or felt his way to his political conclusions did not interest these voters. They saw many men of the highest intelligence and ability opposing the democracy on the income tax, trust control, and other measures where class lines were sometimes drawn; and they concluded that the intelligentsia were not always the safest judges where class decisions must be made. Character and courage and persistence gave him the strength that others gained from other sources, not so readily open to him. Bryan was the prophet and priest of millions, although they did not make him their king. What his enemies could not understand was that the people are as much interested in knowing about their leader's heart as in knowing about his head, and that sympathy no less than intelligence plays its part in the great process of popular control.

H. L. Mencken: IN MEMORIAM: W. J. B.

HAS it been duly marked by historians that the late William Jennings Bryan's last secular act on this globe of sin was to catch flies? A curious detail, and not without its sardonic overtones. He was the most sedulous fly-catcher in American history, and in many ways the most successful. His quarry, of course, was not *Musca domestica* but *Homo neandertalensis*. For forty years he tracked it with coo and bellow, up and down the rustic backways of the Republic. Wherever the flambeaux of Chautauqua smoked and guttered, and the bilge of

Reprinted from *Prejudices* by H. L. Mencken, by permission of Alfred A. Knopf, Inc. Copyright 1926 by Alfred A. Knopf, Inc.

Idealism ran in the veins, and Baptist pastors demmed the brooks with the sanctified, and men gathered who were weary and heavy laden, and their wives who were full of Peruna and as fecund as the shad (*Alosa sapidissima*) — there the indefatigable Jennings set up his traps and spread his bait. He knew every country town in the South and West, and he could crowd the most remote of them to suffocation by simply winding his horn. The city proletariat, transiently flustered by him in 1896, quickly penetrated his buncombe and would have no more of him; the cockney gallery jeered him at every Democratic national convention for twenty-five years. But out where the grass grows high, and the horned cattle dream away the lazy afternoons, and men still fear the powers and principalities of the air — out there between the corn-rows he held his old puissance to the end. There was no need of beaters to drive in his game. The news that he was coming was enough. For miles the flivver dust would choke the roads. And when he rose at the end of the day to discharge his Message there would be such breathless attention, such a rapt and enchanted ecstasy, such a sweet rustle of amens as the world had not known since Johann fell to Herod's ax.

There was something peculiarly fitting in the fact that his last days were spent in a one-horse Tennessee village, and that death found him there. The man felt at home in such simple and Christian scenes. He liked people who sweated freely, and were not debauched by the refinements of the toilet. Making his progress up and down the Main street of little Dayton, surrounded by gaping primates from the upland valleys of the Cumberland Range, his coat laid aside, his bare arms and hairy chest shining damply, his bald head sprinkled with dust — so accoutred and on display he was obviously happy. He liked getting up early in the morning, to the tune of cocks crowing on the dunghill. He liked the heavy, greasy victuals of the farmhouse kitchen. He liked country lawyers, country pastors, all country people. He liked the country sounds and country smells. I believe that this liking was sincere — perhaps the only sincere thing in the man. His nose showed no uneasiness when a hillman in faded overalls and hickory shirt accosted him on the street, and besought him for light upon some mystery of Holy Writ. The simian gabble of the cross-roads was not gabble to him, but wisdom of an occult and superior sort. In the presence of city folks he was palpably uneasy. Their clothes, I suspect, annoyed him, and he was suspicious of their too delicate manners. He knew all the while that they were laughing at him — if not at his baroque theology, then at least at his alpaca pantaloons. But the yokels never laughed at him. To them he was not the huntsman but the prophet, and toward the end, as he gradually forsook mundane politics for more ghostly concerns, they began to elevate him in their hierarchy. When he died he was the peer of Abraham. His old enemy, Wilson, aspiring to the same white and shining robe, came down with a thump. But Bryan made the grade. His place in Tennessee hagiography is secure. If the village barber saved any of his hair, then it is curing gall-stones down there today.

But what label will he bear in more urbane regions? One, I fear, of a far less flattering kind. Bryan lived too long, and descended too deeply into the mud, to be taken seriously hereafter by fully literate men, even of the kind who write schoolbooks. There was a scattering of sweet words in his funeral notices, but it was no more than a response to conventional sentimentality. The best verdict the most romantic editorial writer could dredge up, save in the humorless South, was to the general effect that his imbecilities were excused by his earnestness — that under his clowning, as under that of the juggler of Notre Dame, there was the zeal of a steadfast soul. But this was apology, not praise; precisely the same thing might be said of Mary Baker G. Eddy, the late Czar Nicholas, or Czolgosz. The truth is that even Bryan's sincerity will probably yield to what is called, in other fields, definite criticism. Was he sincere when he opposed imperialism in the Philippines, or when he fed it with deserving Democrats in Santo Domingo? Was he sincere when he tried to shove the Prohibitionist under the table, or when he seized their banner and began to lead them with loud whoops? Was he sincere when he bellowed against war, or when he dreamed of himself as a tin-soldier in uniform, with a grave reserved among the generals? Was he sincere when he denounced the late John W. Davis, or when he swallowed Davis? Was he sincere when he fawned over Champ Clark, or when he betrayed Clark? Was he sincere when he pleaded for tolerance in New York, or when he bawled for the faggot and the stake in Tennessee?

This talk of sincerity, I confess, fatigues me. If the fellow was sincere, then so was P. T. Barnum. The word is disgraced and degraded by such uses. He was, in fact, a charlatan, a mountebank, a zany without shame or dignity. His career brought him into contact with the first men of his time; he preferred the company of rustic ignoramuses. It was hard to believe, watching him at Dayton, that he had traveled, that he had been received in civilized societies, that he had been a high officer of state. He seemed only a poor clod like those around him, deluded by a childish theology, full of an almost pathological hatred of all learning, all human

dignity, all beauty, all fine and noble things. He was a peasant come home to the barnyard. Imagine a gentleman, and you have imagined everything that he was not. What animated him from end to end of his grotesque career was simply ambition — the ambition of a common man to get his hands upon the collar of his superiors, or failing that, to get his thumb into their eyes. He was born with a roaring voice, and it had the trick of inflaming half-wits. His whole career was devoted to raising those half-wits against their betters, that he himself might shine. His last battle will be grossly misunderstood if it is thought of as a mere exercise in fanaticism — that is, if Bryan the Fundamentalist Pope is mistaken for one of the bucolic Fundamentalists. There was more in it than that, as everyone knows who saw him on the field. What moved him, at bottom, was simply hatred of the city men who had laughed at him so long, and brought him at last to so tatterdemalion an estate. He lusted for revenge upon them. He yearned to lead the anthropoid rabble against them, to punish them for their execution upon him by attacking the very vitals of their civilization. He went far beyond the bounds of any merely religious frenzy, however inordinate. When he began denouncing the notion that man is a mammal even some of the hinds at Dayton were agape. And when, brought upon Darrow's cruel hook, he writhed and tossed in a very fury of malignancy, bawling against the baldest elements of sense and decency like a man frantic — when he came to that tragic climax of his striving there were snickers among the hinds as well as hosannas.

Upon that hook, in truth, Bryan committed suicide, as a legend as well as in the body. He staggered from the rustic court ready to die, and he staggered from it ready to be forgotten, save as a character in a third-rate farce, witless and in poor taste. It was plain to everyone who knew him, when he came to Dayton, that his great days were behind him — that, for all the fury of his hatred, he was now definitely an old man, and headed at last for silence. There was a vague, unpleasant manginess about his appearance; he somehow seemed dirty, though a close glance showed him as carefully shaven as an actor, and clad in immaculate linen. All the hair was gone from the dome of his head, and it had begun to fall out, too, behind his ears, in the obscene manner of the late Samuel Gompers. The resonance had departed from his voice; what was once a bugle blast had become reedy and quavering. Who knows that, like Demosthenes, he had a lisp? In the old days, under the magic of his eloquence, no one noticed it. But when he spoke at Dayton it was always audible.

When I first encountered him, on the sidewalk in front of the office of the rustic lawyers who were his associates in the Scopes case, the trial was yet to begin, and so he was still expansive and amiable. I had printed in the *Nation,* a week or so before, an article arguing that the Tennessee anti-evolution law, whatever its wisdom, was at least constitutional — that the rustics of the State had a clear right to have their progeny taught whatever they chose, and kept secure from whatever knowledge violated their superstitions. The old boy professed to be delighted with the argument, and gave the gaping bystanders to understand that I was a publicist of parts. Not to be outdone, I admired the preposterous country shirt that he wore — sleeveless and with the neck cut very low. We parted in the manner of two ambassadors. But that was the last touch of amiability that I was destined to see in Bryan. The next day the

battle joined and his face became hard. By the end of the week he was simply a walking fever. Hour by hour he grew more bitter. What the Christian Scientists call malicious animal magnetism seemed to radiate from him like heat from a stove. From my place in the courtroom, standing upon a table, I looked directly down upon him, sweating horribly and pumping his palm-leaf fan. His eyes fascinated me; I watched them all day long. They were blazing points of hatred. They glittered like occult and sinister gems. Now and then they wandered to me, and I got my share, for my reports of the trial had come back to Dayton, and he had read them. It was like coming under fire.

Thus he fought his last fight, thirsting savagely for blood. All sense departed from him. He bit right and left, like a dog with rabies. He descended to demagogy so dreadful that his very associates at the trial table blushed. His one yearning was to keep his yokels heated up — to lead his forlorn mob of imbeciles against the foe. That foe, alas, refused to be alarmed. It insisted upon seeing the whole battle as a comedy. Even Darrow, who knew better, occasionally yielded to the prevailing spirit. One day he lured poor Bryan into the folly I have mentioned: his astounding argument against the notion that man is a mammal. I am glad I heard it, for otherwise I'd never believe in it. There stood the man who had been thrice a candidate for the Presidency of the Republic — there he stood in the glare of the world, uttering stuff that a boy of eight would laugh at! The artful Darrow led him on: he repeated it, ranted for it, bellowed it in his cracked voice. So he was prepared for the final slaughter. He came into life a hero, a Galahad, in bright and shining armor. He was passing out a poor mountebank.

The chances are that history will put

the peak of democracy in America in his time; it has been on the downward curve among us since the campaign of 1896. He will be remembered perhaps, as its supreme impostor, the *reductio ad absurdum* of its pretension. Bryan came very near being President. In 1896, it is possible, he was actually elected. He lived long enough to make patriots thank the inscrutable gods for Harding, even for Coolidge. Dullness has got into the White House, and the smell of cabbage boiling, but there is at least nothing to compare to the intolerable buffoonery that went on in Tennessee. The President of the United States may be an ass, but he at least doesn't believe that the earth is square, and that witches should be put to death, and that Jonah swallowed the whale. The Golden Text is not painted weekly on the White House wall, and there is no need to keep ambassadors waiting while Pastor Simpson, of Smithville, prays for rain in the Blue Room. We have escaped something— by a narrow margin, but still we have escaped.

That is, so far. The Fundamentalists, once apparently sweeping all before them, now face minorities prepared for battle even in the South — here and there with some assurance of success. But it is too early, it seems to me, to send the firemen home; the fire is still burning on many a far-flung hill, and it may begin to roar again at any moment. The evil that men do lives after them. Bryan, in his malice, started something that will not be easy to stop. In ten thousand country towns his old heelers, the evangelical pastors, are propagating his gospel, and everywhere the yokels are ready for it. When he disappeared from the big cities,

the big cities made the capital error of assuming that he was done for. If they heard of him at all, it was only as a crimp for real-estate speculators — the heroic foe of the unearned increment hauling it in with both hands. He seemed preposterous, and hence harmless. But all the while he was busy among his old lieges, preparing for a *jacquerie* that should floor all his enemies at one blow. He did his job competently. He had vast skill at such enterprises. Heave an egg out of a Pullman window, and you will hit a Fundamentalist almost everywhere in the United States to-day. They swarm in the country towns, inflamed by their *shamans*, and with a saint, now, to venerate. They are thick in the mean streets behind the gas-works. They are everywhere where learning is too heavy a burden for mortal minds to carry, even vague, pathetic learning on tap in little red schoolhouses. They march with the Klan, with the Christian Endeavor Society, with the Junior Order of the United American Mechanics, with the Epworth League, with all the rococo bands that poor and unhappy folk organize to bring some light of purpose into their lives. They have had a thrill, and they are ready for more.

Such is Bryan's legacy to his country. He couldn't be President, but he could at least help magnificently in the solemn business of shutting off the Presidency from every intelligent and self-respecting man. The storm, perhaps, won't last long, as time goes in history. It may help, indeed, to break up the democratic delusion, now already showing weakness, and so hasten its own end. But while it lasts it will blow off some roofs.

Henry S. Commager: WILLIAM JENNINGS BRYAN

TOWARD the end of his life — a life filled with great disappointments and greater achievements — William Jennings Bryan sat down to write his Memoirs. Unhesitatingly, he began:

"I was born in the greatest of all ages. I was born a member of the greatest of all races. I was born a citizen of the greatest of all lands. It was a gift of priceless value to see the light in beloved America, and to live under the greatest of the republics of history."

And he meant it too. This was no mere rhetorical flourish, no appeal for the patriotic vote. It was a confession of faith. That faith was intuitive, to be sure, but it was not blind. It was rather reasoned and undismayed. For no statesman of his generation was a harsher critic of those social and economic conditions that seemed to threaten American democracy, half a century ago, than was Bryan, but none was more sure that democracy would triumph over those threats.

And none, it may be added, better understood the nature of democracy. That understanding was both an inheritance and an achievement — something be had been born to, something he had come to through experience. For more fully than any man of his time he summed up, in himself, the American character. Everything about him illustrated that quality which justified his title, "The Great Commoner." Born in a small farming town in southern Illinois — appropriately named Salem — he came from mixed Scotch, Irish and English stock, from both North and South. One of his parents was Bap-

tist, one Methodist; he himself joined the Presbyterian Church. For generations his family had participated in that westward movement which is part of the American epic — from tidewater Virginia to the Valley, from the Valley to the banks of the Ohio, from the Ohio to the Mississippi; he himself continued the process by moving out to what was then the frontier in Nebraska. He attended a small denominational college, studied law, dabbled in politics, and finally found himself in the championship of a great popular cause.

Bryan's career is familiar enough: how he identified himself with the agrarian crusade sweeping the West like a prairie fire; how, at the age of thirty, he went to Congress and won fame fighting for the income tax, tariff reform, and — above all — free silver; how when the Cleveland administration failed the farmers, he captured control of the Democratic organization, cemented an alliance with the Populists, and pledged the party to a program of reform; how at the Chicago convention of 1896 he stirred the delegates to a frenzy of enthusiasm with his great Cross of Gold oration and himself won the nomination to the presidency; how he waged "the first battle" like a crusade, sweeping the length and breadth of the land, inspiring men everywhere with a new faith in democracy; how, defeated by Mark Hanna and his millions, he held control of the Democratic organization and received the nomination again in 1900; how through eight years of defeat he retained the affection of his followers, went down to defeat again in 1908, and was powerful enough still to dictate the nomination of Woodrow Wilson in 1912. It is a spectacular story, a story without parallel in American political history.

For defeated candidates are usually forgotten and lost causes relegated to historical oblivion, but Bryan was not forgotten and the causes which seemed lost triumphed in the end. He refused to acknowledge defeat, not out of vanity or ambition, but because he was sure that the causes which he championed were right, and sure that right would triumph in the end. And, right or not, most of them did. Few statesmen have ever been more fully vindicated by history. Item by item the program which Bryan had consistently espoused, from the early nineties on into the new century, was written onto the statute books — written into law by those who had denounced and ridiculed it. Call the list of the reforms: government control of currency and of banking, government regulation of railroads, telegraph and telephone, trust regulation, the eight-hour day, labor reforms, the prohibition of injunctions in labor disputes, the income tax, tariff reform, anti-imperialism, the initiative, the referendum, woman suffrage, temperance, international arbitration. These were not all original with Bryan, but it was Bryan who championed them in season and out, who kept them steadily in the political forefront, who held his party firmly to their advocacy.

And he did this with extraordinary astuteness, with consummate ability. For few men have ever been more admirably equipped for political leadership than was the Great Commoner. Tall, handsome, with open countenance, he was a commanding figure on the platform, and when he lifted his voice it was like a whole chorus of heavenly voices. This was nature's greatest gift to him — a voice so melodious, so vibrant, that it cast a spell over his auditors. But he had more than a personality, more than a voice. He was always in command of his subject as well as of his audience, he was wily in defense and audacious in attack, he had endless courage. He had, too, that sense for the jugular vein which is one of the marks of the great strategist — an ability to go to the heart of a matter, to clarify it and simplify it. And with all this went a winning friendliness, loyalty to supporters, a homeliness of speech and a democracy of manners that endeared him to his followers and, in time, even to his enemies.

Yet even this record does not fully explain Bryan's hold on the American people or the unique position which he occupies in our history. For it was his qualities of character rather than his political astuteness that won for him such loyalty as no other leader of his own generation could command — such loyalty as no other American between Clay and Franklin Roosevelt has commanded. Irreproachable in private and professional life, his career was characterized throughout by utter integrity, unqualified sincerity, passionate conviction, courageous consistency, faith in the wisdom of the common man and in the processes of democracy, religious belief in the identity of morals and politics, and an unalterable assurance that the right must eventually triumph over the wrong.

For to Bryan politics was, in the last analysis, a matter of morals. Deeply religious, he tested all issues by moral standards which were to him rigid and unqualified. If he thought a policy, a program, right, he would take it up, and he fought the good fight for many causes that seemed to be lost causes. He had, perhaps, an oversimple view of the world in which he lived, and his standards of right and wrong were emotional and personal rather than intellectual. But in the end he trusted not so much his own judgment as the judgment of the plain people. And this was in the American tradition.

It is for his qualities of character, indeed, that Bryan will be remembered — remembered when the particular causes which he argued are forgotten and the incomparable eloquence with which he argued them echoes only dimly in the memories of old men. For it was not so much that his character was magnanimous — which it was — as that it was so representative of the most typical aspects of American character of that generation.

For Bryan was the last great spokesman of the America of the nineteenth century — of the America of the Middle West and the South, the America of the farm and the country town, the America that read its Bible and went to Chautauqua, distrusted the big city and Wall Street, believed in God and the Declaration of Independence. He was, himself, one of these people. He thought their thoughts, and he spoke the words they were too inarticulate to speak. Above all, he fought their battles. He never failed to raise his voice against injustice, he never failed to believe that in the end justice would be done. Others of his generation served special interests or special groups — the bankers, the railroads, the manufacturers, the officeholders; he looked upon the whole population as his constituency. Others were concerned with the getting of office or of gain; he was zealous to advance human welfare. And when the Blaines and the Hills, the Platts and the Quays, the Hannas and the Forakers are relegated to deserved oblivion, the memory of Bryan will be cherished by the people in whom he had unfaltering faith.

Richard Hofstadter:

THE DEMOCRAT AS REVIVALIST

A man can be born again; the springs of life can be cleansed instantly. . . .
If this is true of one, it can be true of any number. Thus, a nation can be born
in a day if the ideals of the people can be changed.

WILLIAM JENNINGS BRYAN

THOSE who know American revivalism are familiar with the story of the skeptic who comes to the camp meeting to scoff and stays to be converted. Bryan's great "Cross of Gold" speech at the Democratic convention of 1896 had the same galvanic effect. One of his followers who was sitting in the gallery reported the behavior of a near-by gold Democrat who had been sneering at every friendly reference to the silver cause. When Bryan finished his appeal the gold Democrat "lost

Reprinted from *The American Political Tradition* by Richard Hofstadter, by permission of Alfred A. Knopf, Inc. Copyright 1948 by Alfred A. Knopf, Inc.

control of himself and literally grabbed hold of me and pulled me up from a sitting to a standing position on my chair. He yelled at me, 'Yell, for God's sake, yell,' as Bryan closed his speech."

The Great Commoner was a circuit-riding evangelist in politics; the "Cross of Gold" speech, with its religious imagery, its revivalist fervor, its electric reaction upon the audience, was a miniature of his career. Many who laughed at the gospel of his first years in politics came in time to accept much of it as commonplace. Bryan himself, emerging suddenly from obscurity at an hour when the people were in an angry mood, framing his message for a simple constituency nursed in evangelical Protestantism and knowing little literature but the Bible, helped to lead a Great Awakening which swept away much of the cynicism and apathy that had been characteristic of American politics for thirty years.

Bryan was equally at home in religion and politics. In his lecture "The Prince of Peace," which he gave many times and in almost every corner of the world, he declared:

I am interested in the science of government, but I am more interested in religion. .... I enjoy making a political speech . . . but I would rather speak on religion than on politics. I commenced speaking on the stump when I was only twenty, but I commenced speaking in the church six years earlier — and I shall be in the church even after I am out of politics.

Unfortunately Bryan's political leadership and social philosophy were as crude as the theology of his evangelical brethren.

Charles Willis Thompson once remarked that "Bryan's hold on the West lay in the fact that he was himself the average man of a large part of that country; he did not merely resemble that average man, he was that average man." In this Bryan was different from the other great leaders of the Progressive era. Theodore Roosevelt, with his leisure-class background and tastes, Wilson with his professorial reserve, La Follette with his lonely stubbornness and his craftsmanlike interest in the technical details of reform, were singular men. They sensed popular feelings; Bryan embodied them.

Bryan's typical constituent was the long-suffering staple farmer of the West and South. This farmer had broken the prairie or survived the rigors of Reconstruction. His wheat or cotton had fed and clothed the growing industrial population of the cities; exported to Europe, his produce had bought the foreign capital that financed American industrial expansion. For thirty years, since 1865, he had kept his eyes on the general price level, watching it sink downward almost without interruption until at last the dollar had trebled in value. This meant slow agony for the farmer; he was a debtor, and his long-term debts were appreciating intolerably. A debt that he could have paid in 1865 with 1,000 bushels of wheat now cost him 3,000 bushels. To one who owes money and finds it hard to come by, economic hardship appears in its simplest guise as a shortage of money. If money was scarce, the farmer concluded, then the logical thing was to increase the money supply. The silver campaign of 1896 was a struggle between those who wanted money cheap and those who wanted it dear.

But in 1896 free silver ranked among the heresies with free love. Except in the farm country, wherever men of education and substance gathered together it was held beneath serious discussion. Economists in the universities were against it; preachers were against it; writers of editorials were against it. For almost forty years after the campaign was over, the single gold standard remained a fixed star in the firmament of economic orthodoxy, to doubt which was not merely wrong but dishonest. (As late as 1933, when Franklin D. Roosevelt took the United States off the gold standard, Lewis W. Douglas was heard to moan: "Well, this is the end of Western civilization.")

In fact, however, the logic of the silver inflationists was not so wrongheaded as Bryan's orthodox contemporaries believed. Some eminent authorities look back upon the single gold standard as a vicious *idee fixe*,[1] and few will deny that there was a profound need for currency reform in 1896. The farmers were indeed being milked by the interests, in part through contraction of the currency. Accused during the election campaign of fighting for a dishonest dollar, Bryan had by far the better of the argument when he replied that "A dollar approaches honesty as its purchasing power approaches stability."

But free-silverites went on to the disastrous conclusion that currency was the great cause of their miseries, and that currency reform would end them. The many ways in which farmers were victimized by tariffs, railroads, middlemen, speculators, warehousers, and monopolistic producers of farm equipment were all but forgotten; yet these things had been subjects of much sound agitation in the Bryan country not long before; to revive them would have been neither novel nor

strange. In 1892, before the depression brought popular discontents to fever pitch, General James B. Weaver, campaigning on a well-rounded platform of reform issues, had polled over a million votes for president on the Populist ticket. The time seemed ripe for a many-sided attack on abuses that had flourished since the Civil War. Instead, the growing demand for free silver so completely overshadowed other things in the minds of the people as to fix them on a single issue that was at best superficial. This neglect of other facets of reform caused Henry Demarest Lloyd, one of the most intelligent and principled reform spokesmen, to complain:

Free silver is the cow-bird of the reform movement. It waited until the nest had been built by the sacrifices and labour of others, and then it laid its eggs in it, pushing out the others which lie smashed on the ground.

In defense of the free-silver politicians it must be said that they only stressed the issue that the farmers themselves greeted most responsively. "During the campaign of 1892," writes John D. Hicks in *The Populist Revolt*, "the Populists had learned that of all the planks in their platform the silver plank had the widest appeal." And not only to the farmers — it was the only fund-raising issue the Bryan-Altgeld Democrats had; it attracted the Western silver-mineowners who, eager to enlarge their market, gave liberally to the cause, distributed 125,000 copies of W. H. Harvey's plausible free-silver pamphlet, *Coin's Financial School*, and supplied Bryan with most of his meager campaign resources.

Bryan was content to stress free silver to the exclusion of everything else, and thus to freeze the popular cause at its lowest level of understanding. No one can read his campaign speeches in *The*

---

[1] John Maynard Keynes found in the gold standard one of the major causes of the modern world tragedy. In *The General Theory of Employment, Interest, and Money* he stated: "Under the system of domestic *laissez faire* and an international gold standard such as was orthodox in the latter half of the nineteenth century, there was no means open to a government whereby to mitigate economic distress at home except through the competitive struggle for markets."

First Battle without being struck by the way the free-silver obsession elbowed all other questions out of the way. It was the only time in the history of the Republic when a candidate ran for the presidency on the strength of a monomania. At Hartford Bryan asserted warmly: "Of all the instrumentalities which have been conceived by the mind of man for transferring the bread which one man earns to another man who does not earn it, I believe the gold standard is the greatest." In the "Cross of Gold" speech he claimed that "when we have restored the money of the Constitution all other necessary reforms will be possible; but . . . until this is done there is no other reform that can be accomplished."

There seems to have been an element of expediency in Bryan's original acceptance of free silver. "I don't know anything about free silver," he told an audience during his campaign for Congress in 1892. "The people of Nebraska are for free silver and I am for free silver. I will look up the arguments later." Many other politicians have gone through just such an intellectual process, but Bryan's simplicity was unique: he saw nothing to be ashamed of in such a confession. The cause of the people was just; therefore their remedies must be sound; his duty was simply to look up the arguments. That he came to believe earnestly in free silver can hardly be questioned, for his capacity to convince himself, probably the only exceptional thing about his mind, was boundless. "It is a poor head," he once declared, "that cannot find plausible reason for doing what the heart wants to do."

"Of all the men I have seen at close range in thirty-one years of newspaper service," Oswald Garrison Villard has written, "Mr. Bryan seemed to me the most ignorant." The Commoner's heart was filled with simple emotions, but his mind was stocked with equally simple ideas. Presumably he would have lost his political effectiveness if he had learned to look at his supporters with a critical eye, but his capacity for identifying himself with them was costly, for it gave them not so much leadership as expression. He spoke for them so perfectly that he never spoke to them. In his lifelong stream of impassioned rhetoric he communicated only what they already believed.

If Bryan failed to advance a well-rounded program for his farm followers in 1896, he did still less for labor. Aside from one uninspiring address in which he assailed government by injunction — a nod to the Pullman strikers — he did not go far out of his way to capitalize the bitter working-class discontent of the campaign year. Subsequently he was friendly toward labor, but he never sponsored a positive program of labor legislation, and it is doubtful that he had any clear conception of the trials of working-class existence. When he first ran for Congress, he told an audience of farmers that he was "tired of hearing about laws made for the benefit of men who work in shops." In 1896 he won the support of the A. F. of L., then a struggling organization of some 270,000 members, although such labor leaders as Gompers were well aware that "the cause of our ills lies far deeper than the question of gold or silver." In Mark Hanna's estimation Bryan's appeal was too narrow: "He's talking Silver all the time, and that's where we've got him." Bryan ran stronger in the industrial cities of the East than he did in the East generally, but his labor support was too weak to win him any of the heavily populated states.

Bryan's social philosophy, which can be reconstructed from speeches made from 1892 to 1896, was not a grave departure from the historic ideology of the

Democratic Party. Protesting against the drift of government from the popular will, he set down his faith in Jeffersonian principles in the most forthright terms:

> I assert that the people of the United States . . . have sufficient patriotism and sufficient intelligence to sit in judgment on every question which has arisen or which will arise, no matter how long our government will endure. The great political questions are in their final analysis great moral questions, and it requires no extended experience in the handling of money to enable a man to tell right from wrong.

The premise from which Bryan argued was that social problems are essentially moral — that is to say, religious. It was inconceivable that the hardworking, Bible-reading citizenry should be inferior in moral insight to the cynical financiers of the Eastern cities. Because they were, as Bryan saw it, better people, they were better moralists, and hence better economists. In after years when he bustled to the support of the anti-evolution laws with the argument that he was defending the democracy of Tennessee, he was simply carrying this variety of political primitivism to its logical end.

The second principle of Bryan's philosophy was summarized in the old Jacksonian motto that he often quoted: "Equal rights to all and special privileges to none." Like the men of 1828, Bryan felt that he represented a cause that was capable of standing on its own feet without special assistance from the government. The majority of the people, he declaimed, who produced the nation's wealth in peace and rallied to its flag in war, asked for nothing from the government but "even-handed justice." "It is the duty of government to protect all from injustice and to do so without partiality for any one or any class."

Several writers have argued that Bryanism marked the beginning of the end of laissez-faire in the United States, but this is true only in the most indirect and attenuated sense. The Democratic platform of 1896 called for no sweeping restrictions of private enterprise; none of its planks required serious modification of the economic structure through government action.[2] Most of its demands, on the contrary, can be summed up in the expression: "Hands off." The call for a return to bimetallism was a call for the removal of a restriction on silver coinage imposed as late as 1873, not for some thoroughly novel policy. The labor planks asked only that the federal government keep its hands off labor disputes and leave them to state authority — a victory for John P. Altgeld over Grover Cleveland. The income-tax plank was not accounted a means of redistributing wealth on any considerable scale, but merely of forcing the plutocracy to pay for its own services. It was the great merchant, not the farmer, who needed a navy, cried Bryan, echoing the Jeffersonians of old; it was the capitalist, not the poor man, who wanted a standing army "to supplement the local government in protecting his property when he enters into a contest with his employees." Then let the merchant and the capitalist pay their share in maintaining the army and navy. The spirit of the agrarians, throughout defensive rather than aggressive, was aptly expressed by Mary E. Lease when she said that the people were "at bay," and by Bryan himself when he proclaimed: "We do not come as aggressors. . . . We are fighting

[2] The Populist platform, which included proposals for unemployment relief, public works, and government ownership, was more positive in its demands. Bryan deftly dissociated himself, without being too specific, by stating that there were some planks in the Populist platform of which he did not approve.

in defense of our homes, our families and our posterity."

In Bryan's mind the purpose of "the first battle" was to preserve classic American individualism. In one of the most frequently quoted passages of the "Cross of Gold" speech he tried to assimilate the cause of the people to American traditions of enterprise — to restore it, in effect, to respectability by underlining its bourgeois aspirations:

When you come before us and tell us that we are to disturb your business interests, we reply that you have disturbed our business interests by your course. We say to you that you have made the definition of a business man too limited in its application. The man who is employed for wages is as much a business man as his employer. The attorney in a country bank is as much a business man as the corporation counsel in a great metropolis; a merchant at the crossroads store is as much a business man as the merchant of New York; the farmer who goes forth in the morning and toils all day — who begins in the spring and toils all summer — and who by the application of brawn and muscle to the natural resources of the country, creates wealth, is as much a business man as the man who goes upon the Board of Trade and bets upon the price of grain.

When he came to New York to deliver his acceptance address he declared in words strikingly similar to Jackson's bank message:

Our campaign has not for its object the reconstruction of society. We cannot insure to the vicious the fruits of a virtuous life; we would not invade the home of the provident in order to supply the wants of the spendthrift; we do not propose to transfer the rewards of industry to the lap of indolence. Property is and will remain the stimulus to endeavor and the compensation for toil. We believe, as asserted in the Declaration of Independence, that all men are created equal; but that does not mean that all men are or can be equal in possessions, in ability, or in merit; it simply means that all shall stand equal before the law. . . .

After one hundred years of change in society the Jeffersonian-Jacksonian philosophy was intact. To those who accept that philosophy, this will appear as steadfastness of faith; to those who reject it, as inflexibility of mind.

II

Ridiculed and condemned by all Eastern Respectability in 1896, denounced as an anarchist, a socialist, a subverter of religion and morals, the victim of every device that wealth and talents could bring to bear, Bryan has gained a place among the celebrated American rebels. But in an important psychological sense he was never a rebel at all — and this is a clue to the torpor of his mind. What was lacking in him was a sense of alienation. He never felt the excitement of intellectual discovery that comes with rejection of one's intimate environment. The revolt of the youth against paternal authority, of the village agnostic against the faith of his tribe, of the artist against the stereotypes of philistine life, of the socialist against the whole bourgeois community — such experiences were not within his ken. Near the end of his life his own party laughed him off the stage, but that came too late to be instructive.

Politicians cannot be expected to have the traits of detached intellectuals, but few men in any phase of life have been so desolately lacking as Bryan in detachment or intellectuality. While he was eager to grapple with his opponents in the political arena, he was incapable of confronting them in the arena of his own mind. His characteristic mental state was not that of a man who has abandoned the assumptions of his society or his class after a searching examination, but rather of one who has been so thoroughly nurtured in a provincial heresy that it has become for him merely another orthodoxy. Colonel House relates that Bryan often told him "that a man who did not believe in the free and unlimited coinage of silver at 16 to 1 was either a fool or a knave." Bryan was rooted in a section of the country where his panaceas were widely taken as gospel; even the substantial citizenry of the West gave him a following. As he complacently observed in *The First Battle* concerning the men who helped him launch the Nebraska Democratic free-silver movement in 1894, "They were all men of standing in the State and most of them men of considerable property." He referred to the East as "the enemy's country." When he went to battle for the Western farmer, therefore, it was not in the spirit of a domestic quarrel in which one's object is to persuade, but of a war against a foreign power in which an exchange of views is impossible. He could no more analyze the issues of his day than the Confederates could realize the obsolescence of slavery.

Intellectually, Bryan was a boy who never left home. His father, Silas Bryan, was a Baptist and a Democrat of Southern origin, who carved out a successful career in the "Egypt" section of Illinois, became a judge in the state courts, owned a large house, and provided his family with the stale culture and niggardly comfort that usually result when ample means are used to achieve Puritan ends. In 1872, when Bryan was twelve, Silas Bryan ran for Congress with the endorsement of the Greenback Party. The father believed in the supremacy of the Anglo-Saxon race, the value of education as an instrument of success, democratic opportunity, the God of the Old Testament, and an ex-

panded currency. The son never found reason to question these convictions: there was no ideological tension in the Bryan household. William Jennings did break with his father's church to join the Presbyterians, abandoning his ambition to become a Baptist minister because he was frightened by the strenuous dunking of the baptismal ceremony, but he learned that his conversion had hurt Silas Bryan's feelings only long after his father was dead.

From his father's home Bryan was sent to Whipple Academy and Illinois College at Jacksonville, Illinois. His six years there did nothing to awaken his mind. The faculty of Illinois College consisted of eight men, and its curriculum carried no subject except mathematics and classics beyond an introductory course. During his years of attendance Bryan withdrew eighteen books from the college library (which was closed to students all but a few hours of the day), and they were chiefly fiction. (Bryan especially liked the novels of Charles Dickens.) The president of the college, Julian Monson Sturtevant, was the author of a textbook, *Economics*, which defended free trade and bimetallism. "The President of the College," Bryan declaimed happily, "is for free trade, our ex-President is for free trade, and I *myself* am for free trade." After what Bryan had heard in his father's home and absorbed from Sturtevant, the protective tariff and monometallism seemed outlandish.

For two years after leaving college Bryan read law at the Union College of Law in Chicago and in the office of Lyman Trumbull, after which he returned to Jacksonville, married the daughter of a prosperous storekeeper, and for five years practiced law without distinction. Smarting with realization of his mediocrity as a lawyer, Bryan fled westward and settled in Lincoln, Nebraska, where he soon edged into politics under the protective wing of J. Sterling Morton, the Democratic political agent of the railroads. He was fond of saying that he had entered politics by accident, but in a franker mood he once confessed: "Certainly from the time I was fifteen years old, I had but one ambition in life, and that was to come to Congress. I studied for it. I worked for it, and everything I did had that object in view."

In 1890, with the backing of the business and liquor interests of Omaha, he won a seat in Congress. Two years later, after many months of arduous study, he made an impressive anti-tariff speech in the House, which focused national attention upon him. Then, quickly perceiving the decline of the tariff as a political issue, and observing the rapid rise of Populism, which was especially strong in his own state, he took up free silver. Nebraska districts had been rearranged; Omaha was no longer in his bailiwick; Bryan now "looked up arguments" on silver as he had on the tariff, negotiated financial backing from the Utah and Colorado silver-mine operators, and won re-election from a more rural constituency. In 1893 he made another spectacular speech in Congress against repeal of the Sherman Silver Purchase Act, of which almost a million copies were distributed by silver-mine-owners. The following year he tried for election to the Senate, but the legislature spurned him, and he turned to an ill-paid position as editor of the Omaha *World-Herald*, which had been procured by his patrons among the silver interests. With cool nerve and considerable skill, he set to work to make the *World-Herald* an instrument of his presidential ambitions, which then seemed fabulously premature to everyone but himself.

Bryan's political career after 1896 was a long, persistent search for an issue comparable in effect to free silver, and an equally persistent campaign to keep himself in the public eye. In 1899 anti-imperialism seemed a likely issue. Democratic and Populist opponents of expansion were planning to block annexation of the Philippines by rejecting the peace treaty with Spain in the Senate. To Bryan, fighting in this way as an organized minority seemed wrong; the people themselves must decide — and the issue must be exploited in a campaign. Assuming that an anti-imperialist platform in 1900 would appeal to the idealism of the American people, as the cause of Cuba had before the war, he managed to persuade just enough Democratic Senators to permit the treaty to pass. He proposed to win a mandate for Philippine independence in the election. This was the most grotesque miscalculation of his life. Anti-imperialism would have been a much more live issue if the treaty had been rejected and the question of annexing the Philippines was still hanging fire. Once the treaty was ratified, the people were quite content to let the matter rest. Bryan found anti-imperialism such a sterile issue during his 1900 campaign that he turned increasingly to others — anti-trust and free silver — but prosperity had returned and he was unable to excite the electorate as before.

Bryan's attempt to revive the stale free-silver issue during the campaign also backfired. The world production of gold, stimulated by the new cyanide extraction process and the discovery of fresh deposits, had risen markedly, and the price level had also gone up, but when followers like the sociologist E. A. Ross pointed out to Bryan that the new gold supplies had relieved the money shortage and undermined the cause of silver, the Commoner was unimpressed. Considerations of practical economics, Ross recalls, meant little to him. "He . . . merely suggested how to parry arguments based upon them brought out by our opponents. . . . I saw that Mr. Bryan was no realist." From a strategic standpoint, Bryan was worse than wrong, he was impractical. By insisting on the free-silver plank in the 1900 platform he may have lost whatever chance he had of winning some of the Eastern states, while he did not need the issue to win the West or the South. "Bryan," quipped Thomas B. Reed, "had rather be wrong than president."

In 1902 Bryan took a trip abroad and observed state ownership of utilities as it was practiced in European countries. Thrown aside by his party in 1904 in favor of the conservative Alton B. Parker, he continued to press for a more radical program, including government ownership and operation of the railways. And yet, after Theodore Roosevelt's overwhelming victory, he visited the Rough Rider at the White House, greeting him with the words: "Some people think I'm a terrible radical, but really I'm not so very dangerous after all." To the New York *Tribune* he wrote: "It is time to call a halt on Socialism in the United States. The movement is going too far." Then in the summer of 1906, returning from a grand tour of the world, he went back to government ownership of railroads. He had now achieved a synthesis: government ownership would be a way of avoiding socialism:

The man who argues that there is an economic advantage in private monopoly is aiding socialism. The socialist, asserting the economic superiority of the monopoly, insists that its benefits shall accrue to the whole

people, and his conclusion cannot be denied if his assertion is admitted. The Democratic party, if I understand its position, denies the economic as well as the political advantage of private monopoly and promises to oppose it wherever it manifests itself. It offers as an alternative competition where competition is possible, and public monopoly wherever circumstances are such as to prevent competition.

Like free silver in 1900, government ownership of railways did not take with the voters. Preparing for his third presidential nomination in 1908, Bryan scurried to haul down his flag, promised that he would not "force government ownership upon the country against the will of the people," and testified in a letter to the *Wall Street Journal* that he was in "no hurry about government ownership." Instead he campaigned on the trust question, proposing a rule-of-thumb system of curbing big business that must have caused apoplexy in hundreds of clubrooms.[3] The campaign was rather listless, and the mammoth Taft beat the Commoner more soundly than McKinley had in 1896 or 1900.

And yet, while Bryan had the smallest percentage of the total vote received by any Democratic candidate except Parker for the past sixty years, his ideas were about to reach the peak of their influence. Theodore Roosevelt, during both his terms, had been appropriating one after another of Bryan's smaller issues. Progressive Democrats, held in cohesion by

[3] According to Bryan's formula, when a corporation engaged in interstate commerce came to control as much as 25 per cent of the business in its field of enterprise it must obtain a federal license; the provisions of this license would guarantee the public against watered stock and prevent the corporation from controlling more than 50 per cent of the traffic in its product or products.

the Bryan influence, were to harass Taft in collaboration with the Progressive Republicans. Finally, in 1912 Bryan was to help swing the Democratic nomination to Woodrow Wilson. The Commoner, always defeated, had, in the course of a sixteen-year quest for issues, effectively turned public attention upon one reform after another; and many of his proposals had had a core of value. Mary Bryan, completing her husband's *Memoirs* in 1925, listed with understandable pride the Bryan projects that had become law: the federal income tax, popular election of United States Senators, publicity in campaign contributions, woman suffrage, a Department of Labor, more stringent railroad regulation, currency reform, and, in the states, the initiative and referendum.

Bryan accepted his perennial defeats with a good humor that seems extraordinary, in the light of the earnestness of his campaigns and the vituperation that was heaped upon him. There is good reason, however, to doubt that at heart he ever really expected to win. He had risen overnight from comparative obscurity to become a major presidential candidate — a thrilling and profoundly gratifying experience. He was grateful that he could run at all, that he could run again, and yet again, that he could earn a good and easy living at the Chautauquas, that he could constantly command national attention, thrill millions with his fine voice, throw a Democratic convention into an uproar with a barbed phrase. For Silas Bryan's son who had once seemed on the verge of failure in the law, this was ample achievement. As prices turned upward and the temper of his following eased, Bryan grew fat and genial, and on occasion passed jests about the futility of his campaigns. It was never success that he demanded, but an audience, and not until audiences began to laugh at him did he

become the bitter and malignant old man of the Scopes trial.

III

When Woodrow Wilson reluctantly appointed him Secretary of State, Bryan held a leading office for the only time in his career and the State Department at last had a head who was committed to oppose imperialism and dollar diplomacy. But those who remembered his earlier career wondered what this might mean in practice. Bryan had been a most eloquent Christian pacifist, and yet when the Spanish War came he had fulfilled his idea of "service" by enlisting in the First Nebraska Volunteers, rising to a colonelcy, and camping with his troops in a sinkhole near Jacksonville, Florida, until the war was over. The inconsistency between his participation in the war and his discipleship of the Prince of Peace seemed not to trouble him. (Paxton Hibben remarked that the Commoner "appeared unable to grasp that the sole business of a soldier is to kill. To Bryan the function of a soldier was to be killed — he saw war a game to be won by sacrifice hits.")

Bryan in power was like Bryan out of power: he made the same well-meant gestures, showed the same willingness under stress or confusion to drop ideas he had once been committed to, the same inability to see things through. His most original enterprise was to promote a series of international arbitration treaties, a task that he undertook with moral earnestness such as had not been seen in his Department for many years. These treaties provided that when disputes arose between contracting parties, there should be a "cooling-off" period to permit animosities to wane, followed by arbitration. He had great hopes for the treaties; they would help materially to dissipate the danger of war. "I believe there will be no war while

I am Secretary of State," he declared fervently in 1913, "and I believe there will be no war so long as I live."

Bryan's inability to hold steadily to a line of principle was nowhere so well illustrated as in his imperialist policies in the Caribbean, where, as Selig Adler has shown, he was "chiefly responsible for a distinct acceleration of American penetration." Wilson, harassed by the Mexican question and the problems of neutrality, gave Bryan a substantially free hand in Caribbean policy, and the former anti-imperialist, in dealing with Nicaragua, Haiti, and Santo Domingo, was fully as aggressive as his Republican predecessors. Root, Knox, or Hay could have been no more nationalistic or jealous of the prerogatives of American capital in the face of foreign penetration. Apropos of the Haitian situation, Bryan wrote to Wilson, April 2, 1915:

As long as the [Haitian] Government is under French or German influence American interests are going to be discriminated against there as they are discriminated against now. . . . The American interests are willing to remain there with a view of purchasing a controlling interest and making the Bank a branch of the American bank . . . providing their Government takes the steps necessary to protect them. . . . I have been reluctant to favor anything that would require an exercise of force there, but there are some things that lead me to believe that it may be necessary to use as much force as may be necessary [*sic*] to compel a supervision which will be effective.

Bryan also wanted to father a sweeping policy of financial intervention in Latin America, which he outlined in two memoranda to Wilson in 1913. He proposed to counteract the influence of European creditors of Latin-American nations by having the United States government go

to their "rescue." The United States would make available the funds necessary for the education, sanitation, and internal development of these nations, and relieve them of the necessity of applying to private financiers in other countries, thus making "absolutely sure our domination of the situation." This would so increase the nation's influence in Latin America "that we could prevent revolutions, promote education, and advance stable and just government." In proposing to wave aside private interests and make economic penetration a state function, Bryan, in the words of Samuel Flagg Bemis, anticipated "the formula of the newer dollar diplomacy of our day." Wilson, however, was not impressed by Bryan's plans.

With the advent 'of the World War Bryan was the one major figure in the Wilson administration who represented a genuinely neutral point of view. A Midwesterner and an old opponent of the international gold power, Bryan did not look at Britain with the soft eyes of the middle- and upper-class East. His great aim was not to further the Allied cause, but to maintain such relations with both sides as would make possible American arbitration. For his persistent criticism of administration policies Wilson's biographer, Ray Stannard Baker, has found him "the statesman of largest calibre" among Wilson's advisers. Urging mediation upon the President in September 1914, Bryan wrote prophetically:

It is not likely that either side will win so complete a victory as to be able to dictate terms, and if either side does win such a victory it will probably mean preparation for another war. It would seem better to look for a more rational basis for peace.

When American bankers brought pressure upon the administration to allow them to make large loans to the Allies, Bryan was primarily responsible for choking off the project. Money, he pointed out, was the worst of all contrabands because it could command all other goods; such economic commitments to the Allies would be inconsistent with the spirit of neutrality and would ultimately lead to war. Events proved him right, but he characteristically refused to hold to his position and quietly gave his consent when it was proposed to jettison his original ban on loans. Just as he had gone back on anti-imperialism, pacifism, and government ownership of railways, so he backed down on the loans question.

It was neither courage nor sincerity but simply steadfast and self-confident intelligence that Bryan lacked. The steady drift of the United States away from neutrality caused him untold anguish. When Wilson began a long train of controversy with Germany by permitting American citizens to travel on British vessels that were likely to be sunk by U-boats, Bryan alone perceived the folly of the stand. The question, as he put it, was "whether an American citizen can, by putting his business above his regard for his country, assume for his own advantage unnecessary risks and thus involve his country in international complications." He also urged acceptance of the German proposal that relaxation of submarine warfare be exchanged for relaxation of the British food blockade against Germany, but the idea received no sympathy in Britain. "Why be shocked," he then asked Wilson, "at the drowning of a few people, if there is to be no objection to starving a nation?" Troubled by Wilson's protests to Germany over the sinking of the Lusitania, he resigned, June 8, 1915.

Bryan decayed rapidly during his closing years. The postwar era found him identified with some of the worst tendencies in American life — prohibition, the crusade against evolution, real-estate speculation, and the Klan. For the sake of his wife's health he moved to Florida, where he became a publicity agent for the real-estate interests, in which capacity his incurable vulgarity stood him in good stead —"What is our vision of what Magic Miami should be?" He collected such magnificent fees for his real-estate promotion and his prohibition lectures that he was able to bequeath a small fortune. His last political appearance took place at the Democratic convention of 1924 in New York City, when the party was racked with conflict over the famous resolution denouncing the Ku Klux Klan by name, and the delegations from the Bryan country were filled with Klan supporters. It was a magnificent opportunity for a man who had read Jefferson on tolerance to give a great lecture on bigotry. Instead, fearing more than anything else a further decline in his influence, Bryan delivered a weal appeal not to rend the "Christian Church" nor destroy party unity. Of the Klan he said: "We can exterminate Ku Kluxism better by recognizing their honesty and teaching them that they are wrong." Fat, balding, in wrinkled clothes, taxed by the heat, bereft of the splendid voice that had made him famous, he was unequal to the merciless heckling from the galleries, and when he descended from the platform after a ludicrous effort to promote compromise candidates, he told Senator Heflin with tears in his eyes that he had never in his life been so humiliated.

When the convention, in a stalemate between Al Smith and William Gibbs McAdoo, nominated John W. Davis, a lawyer for Morgan and Standard Oil, Bryan, who had once scourged the Morgan forces in a party conclave, lent his brother Charles to the Davis ticket as vice-presidential nominee and supported Davis in the campaign. Bryan's old principles were represented that year by Robert M. La Follette on an independent progressive ticket, but La Follette got no support from the man whose followers had so often united with him in Congressional fights. The Commoner could no more think of leaving the Democratic Party than of being converted to Buddhism. He had never failed to support a Democratic nominee. The party, he confessed to the 1924 convention, was the great passion of his life; he owed it an unpayable debt, for it had taken him out of obscurity, a young, penniless man, and had lifted him to exalted heights, three times honoring him with nominations.

But even in the Democratic Party, Bryan knew, his influence was on the wane. He was an agrarian leader, whose strength lay in his appeal to a certain type of Protestant mind in the hinterland; the growing urbanism of the country was submerging him. He was not forgotten by his old followers, but as he wrote an acquaintance in 1923, "the wets are against me and they have the organization and the papers in all the big cities of the north. I cannot get before the public."

As his political power slipped away, Bryan welcomed an opportunity to divert himself with a new crusade and turned with devotion to his first interest. To one correspondent he wrote:

While my power in politics has waned, I think it has increased in religious matters and I have invitations from preachers in all the churches. An evidence of the change is found in the fact that my correspondence in religious subjects is much larger than my correspondence in political subjects. My interest is deeper in religious subjects because I believe that the brute theory has paralyzed

the influence of many of our preachers and undermined the faith of many of our young people in college.

He once explained that he thought himself fit to be a leader in the fight against evolution because he had had a measure of success in his life that would dispel all doubts as to his "mental ability." He began to give lectures to the college youth of the nation bearing the message: "No teacher should be allowed on the faculty of any American university unless he is a Christian."

Bryan's presence for the prosecution at the trial of John Thomas Scopes for teaching evolution in Tennessee surprised no one who had been following his talks. The Scopes trial, which published to the world Bryan's childish conception of religion, also reduced to the absurd his inchoate notions of democracy. His defense of the anti-evolution laws showed that years of political experience had not taught him anything about the limitations of public opinion. The voice of the people was still the voice of God. The ability of the common man to settle every question extended, he thought, to matters of science as well as politics and applied equally well to the conduct of schools as it did to the regulation of railroads or the recall of judges or the gold standard. In prosecuting Scopes the people were merely asserting their right "to have what they want in government, including the kind of education they want." Academic freedom? That right "cannot be stretched as far as Professor Scopes is trying to stretch it. A man cannot demand a salary for saying what his employers do not want said. . . ."

So spoke the aging Bryan, the knight-errant of the oppressed. He closed his career in much the same role as he had begun it in 1896: a provincial politician following a provincial populace in provincial prejudices. From all corners of the country, but especially from the old Bryan territory, came messages of encouragement. "MY DEAR BROTHER BRYAN," wired an admirer from Smackover, Arkansas, "FIGHT THEM EVOLUTIONS UNTIL HELL FREEZES OVER AND THEN GIVE THEM A ROUND ON THE ICE." When a few weeks after the trial's close Bryan's heart gave out, there was profound grief among those who had followed him faithfully from the fight against gold to the fight against the ape. Fiery crosses were burned in his memory, and one of his constituents celebrated him as "the greatest Klansman of our time." A cruel and inaccurate characterization, it underscored the fatal weakness of a man who at sixty-five had long outlived his time.

Vachel Lindsay: BRYAN, BRYAN, BRYAN, BRYAN

The Campaign of Eighteen Ninety-six, as Viewed at the Time by a Sixteen Year Old, etc.

I

In a nation of one hundred fine, mob-hearted, lynching, relenting, repenting millions,
There are plenty of sweeping, swinging, stinging, gorgeous things to shout about
And knock your old blue devils out.

I brag and chant of Bryan, Bryan, Bryan,
Candidate for president who sketched a silver Zion,
The one American Poet who could sing outdoors.
He brought in tides of wonder, of unprecedented splendor,
Wild roses from the plains, that made hearts tender,
All the funny circus silks
Of politics unfurled,
Bartlett pears of romance that were honey at the cores,
And torchlights down the street, to the end of the world.
There were truths eternal in the gab and tittle-tattle.

There were real heads broken in the fustian and the rattle.
There were real lines drawn:
Not the silver and the gold
But Nebraska's cry went eastward against the dour and old,
The mean and cold.

It was eighteen ninety-six, and I was just sixteen
And Altgeld ruled in Springfield, Illinois,
When there came from the sunset Nebraska's shout of joy: —
In a coat like a deacon, in a black Stetson hat
He scourged the elephant plutocrats
With barbed wire from the Platte.
The scales dropped from their mighty eyes.
They saw that summer's moon
A tribe of wonders coming
To a marching tune.

Oh the long horns from Texas,
The jay hawks from Kansas,

The plop-eyed bungaroo and giant
    giassicus,
The varmint, chipmunk, bugaboo,
The horned-toad, prairie-dog and bally-
    hoo,
From all the new-born states arow,
Bidding the eagles of the west fly on,
Bidding the eagles of the west fly on.
The fawn, prodactyl and thing-a-ma-jig,
The rakaboor, the hellangone,
The whangdoodle, batfowl and pig,
The coyote, wild-cat and grizzly in a glow,
In a miracle of health and speed, the
    whole breed abreast,
They leaped the Mississippi, blue border
    of the West,
From the Gulf to Canada, two thousand
    miles long: —
Against the towns of Tubal Cain,
Ah, — sharp was their song.
Against the ways of Tubal Cain, too cun-
    ning for the young,
The long-horn calf, the buffalo and
    wampus gave tongue.

These creatures were defending things
    Mark Hanna never dreamed:
The moods of airy childhood that in
    desert dews gleamed,
The gossamers and whimsies,
The monkeyshines and didoes
Rank and strange
Of the canyons and the range,
The ultimate fantastics
Of the far western slope,
And of prairie schooner children
Born beneath the stars
Beneath falling snows,
Of the babies born at midnight
In the sod huts of lost hope,
With no physician there,
Except a Kansas prayer,
With the Indian raid a howling through
    the air.

And all these in their helpless days
By the dour East oppressed,

Mean paternalism
Making their mistakes for them,
Crucifying half the West,
Till the whole Atlantic coast
Seemed a giant spiders' nest.

And these children and their sons
At last rode through the cactus,
A cliff of mighty cowboys
On the lope,
With gun and rope.
And all the way to frightened Maine the
    old East heard them call,
And saw our Bryan by a mile lead the wall
Of men and whirling flowers and beasts,
The bard and the prophet of them all.
Prairie avenger, mountain lion,
Bryan, Bryan, Bryan, Bryan,
Gigantic troubadour, speaking like a siege
    gun,
Smashing Plymouth Rock with his bould-
    ers from the West,
And just a hundred miles behind, tor-
    nadoes piled across the sky,
Blotting out sun and moon,
A sign on high.
Headlong, dazed and blinking in the
    weird green light,
The scalawags made moan,
Afraid to fight.

II

When Bryan came to Springfield, and
    Altgeld gave him greeting,
Rochester was deserted, Divernon was
    deserted,
Mechanicsburg, Riverton, Chickenbristle,
    Cotton Hill,
Empty: for all Sangamon drove to the
    meeting —
In silver-decked racing cart,
Buggy, buckboard, carryall,
Carriage, phaeton, whatever would haul,
And silver-decked farm-wagons gritted,
    banged and rolled,
With the new tale of Bryan by the iron
    tires told.

The State House loomed afar,
A speck, a hive, a football,
A captive balloon!
And the town was all one spreading wing
   of bunting, plumes, and sunshine,
Every rag and flag, and Bryan picture
   sold,
When the rigs in many a dusty line
Jammed our streets at noon,
And joined the wild parade against the
   power of gold.

We roamed, we boys from High School
With mankind,
While Springfield gleamed,
Silk-lined.
Oh Tom Dines, and Art Fitzgerald,
And the gangs that they could get!
I can hear them yelling yet.
Helping the incantation,
Defying aristocracy,
With every bridle gone,
Ridding the world of the low down mean,
Bidding the eagles of the West fly on,
Bidding the eagles of the West fly on,
We were bully, wild and wooly,
Never yet curried below the knees.
We saw flowers in the air,
Fair as the Pleiades, bright as Orion,
— Hopes of all mankind,
Made rare, resistless, thrice refined.
Oh we bucks from every Springfield
   ward!
Colts of democracy —
Yet time-winds out of Chaos from the
   star-fields of the Lord.

The long parade rolled on. I stood by my
   best girl.
She was a cool young citizen, with wise
   and laughing eyes.
With my necktie by my ear, I was step-
   ping on my dear,
But she kept like a pattern, without a
   shaken curl.
She wore in her hair a brave prairie rose.

Her gold chums cut her, for that was not
   the pose.
No Gibson Girl would wear it in that fresh
   way.
But we were fairy Democrats, and this
   was our day.

The earth rocked like the ocean, the side-
   walk was a deck.
The houses for the moment were lost in
   the wide wreck.
And the bands played strange and
   stranger music as they trailed along.
Against the ways of Tubal Cain,
Ah, sharp was their song!
The demons in the bricks, the demons in
   the grass,
The demons in the bank-vaults peered out
   to see us pass,
And the angels in the trees, the angels in
   the grass,
The angels in the flags, peered out to see
   us pass.
And the sidewalk was our chariot, and the
   flowers bloomed higher,
And the street turned to silver and the
   grass turned to fire,
And then it was but grass, and the town
   was there again,
A place for women and men.

III

Then we stood where we could see
Every band,
And the speaker's stand.
And Bryan took the platform.
And he was introduced.
And he lifted his hand
And cast a new spell.
Progressive silence fell
In Springfield,
In Illinois,
Around the world.
Then we heard these glacial boulders
   across the prairie rolled:

"The people have a right to make their
*   own mistakes. . . .*
You shall not crucify mankind
Upon a cross of gold."

And everybody heard him —
In the streets and State House yard.
And everybody heard him
In Springfield,
In Illinois,
Around and around and around the world,
That danced upon its axis
And like a darling broncho whirled.

IV

July, August, suspense.
Wall Street lost to sense.
August, September, October,
More suspense,
And the whole East down like a wind-
     smashed fence.

Then Hanna to the rescue,
Hanna of Ohio,
Rallying the roller-tops,
Rallying the bucket-shops,
Threatening drouth and death,
Promising manna,
Rallying the trusts against the bawling
     flannelmouth;
Invading misers' cellars,
Tin-cans, socks,
Melting down the rocks,
Pouring out the long green to a million
     workers,
Spondulix by the mountain-load, to stop
     each new tornado,
And beat the cheapskate, blatherskite,
Populistic, anarchistic,
Deacon — desperado.

V

Election night at midnight:
Boy Bryan's defeat.
Defeat of western silver.
Defeat of the wheat.
Victory of letterfiles

And plutocrats in miles
With dollar signs upon their coats,
Diamond watchchains on their vests
And spats on their feet.
Victory of custodians,
Plymouth Rock,
And all that inbred landlord stock.
Victory of the neat.
Defeat of the aspen groves of Colorado
     valleys,
The blue bells of the Rockies,
And blue bonnets of old Texas,
By the Pittsburg alleys.
Defeat of alfalfa and the Mariposa lily.
Defeat of the Pacific and the long
     Mississippi.
Defeat of the young by the old and silly.
Defeat of tornadoes by the poison vats
     supreme.
Defeat of my boyhood, defeat of my
     dream.

VI

Where is McKinley, that respectable
     McKinley,
The man without an angle or a tangle,
Who soothed down the city man and
     soothed down the farmer,
The German, the Irish, the Southerner,
     the Northerner,
Who climbed every greasy pole, and
     slipped through every crack;
Who soothed down the gambling hall, the
     bar-room, the church,
The devil vote, the angel vote, the neutral
     vote,
The desperately wicked, and their victims
     on the rack,
The gold vote, the silver vote, the brass
     vote, the lead vote,
Every vote. . . .

Where is McKinley, Mark Hanna's
     McKinley,
His slave, his echo, his suit of clothes?
Gone to join the shadows, with the pomps
     of that time,

And the flame of that summer's prairie
   rose.

Where is Cleveland whom the Demo-
   cratic platform
Read from the party in a glorious hour?
Gone to join the shadows with pitchfork
   Tillman,
And sledge-hammer Altgeld who wrecked
   his power.

Where is Hanna, bulldog Hanna,
Low-browed Hanna, who said: "Stand
   pat"?
Gone to his place with old Pierpont
   Morgan.
Gone somewhere . . . with lean rat Platt.

Where is Roosevelt, the young dude
   cowboy,

Who hated Bryan, then aped his way?
Gone to join the shadows with mighty
   Cromwell
And tall King Saul, till the Judgment day.

Where is Altgeld, brave as the truth,
Whose name the few still say with tears?
Gone to join the ironies with Old John
   Brown,
Whose fame rings loud for a thousand
   years.

Where is that boy, that Heaven-born
   Bryan,
That Homer Bryan, who sang from the
   West?
Gone to join the shadows with Altgeld the
   Eagle,
Where the kings and the slaves and the
   troubadours rest.

Suggestions for Additional Reading

I. AGRICULTURAL UNREST. The best single volume is John D. Hicks, *The Populist Revolt* (Minneapolis, 1931), which contains a well-arranged bibliographical appendix. An earlier history, Frank L. McVey, *The Populist Movement* (New York, 1896), is valuable for a full listing of contemporary newspaper and magazine material, but is violently anti-Populist. Solon J. Buck, *The Agrarian Crusade* (New Haven, 1920), is a judicious brief chronicle, and the same author has written the standard account of *The Granger Movement, 1870–1880* (Cambridge, 1913), with bibliography. Useful also is Orin G. Libby, "A Study of the Greenback Movement," *Transactions of the Wisconsin Academy* (Madison, 1898), 12: 530–543. Of fundamental importance are Fred A. Shannon, *The Farmer's Last Frontier* (New York, 1945), and two articles by Hallie Farmer, "The Economic Background of Frontier Populism," *Mississippi Valley Historical Review*, 10 (March, 1924), 406–427, and "The Railroads and Frontier Populism," *ibid.*, 13 (December, 1926), 387–397. The statistics compiled by George Frederick Warren in "Prices of Farm Products in the United States," *U. S. Department of Agriculture Bulletin*, No. 99 (Washington, 1921), may be pondered with profit.

The following monographs and general histories give special attention to the plight of the farmer: Nathan Fine, *Labor and Farmer Parties in the United States, 1828–1928* (New York, c. 1928), emphasis on labor; Chester M. Destler, *American Radicalism, 1865–1901* (New Lon-don, Conn., 1946), treats mainly the Labor-Populist alliance in Illinois; Leon W. Fuller, "Colorado's Revolt against Capitalism," *Mississippi Valley Historical Review*, 21 (December, 1934), 365–380; Alex M. Arnett, *The Populist Movement in Georgia* (New York, 1922), presents the Southern angle; Fred Emory Haynes, *Third Party Movements since the Civil War* (Iowa City, 1916), touches Populism lightly; Davis R. Dewey, *National Problems, 1885–1897* (New York, 1907); Charles A. Beard, *Contemporary American History* (New York, 1914); David S. Muzzey, *The United States of America* (2 vols., Boston, 1924), chapters on "The Revolt of the West" and "The Progressive Movement"; Frederic L. Paxson, *The New Nation* (Boston, 1915), *Recent History of the United States* (Boston, 1928), and *When the West Is Gone* (Boston, 1930).

Three books by Populist leaders deserve particular mention: William A. Peffer, *The Farmer's Side* (New York, 1891), a widely read political manual; James B. Weaver, *A Call to Action* (Des Moines, Iowa, 1892), by the Populist candidate for President in 1892; and Henry Demarest Lloyd, *Wealth against Commonwealth* (New York, 1894).

A sampling of contemporary periodicals yields the following suggestive comments and analyses: Frank Drew, "The Present Farmer's Movement," *Political Science Quarterly*, 5 (June, 1891), 282–310; James H. Canfield and others, "A Bundle of Western Letters," *Review of Reviews*, 10 (July, 1894), 42–46, a cross section of local reactions to the Populist program; William V. Allen, "Western Feeling Towards the East," *North American Review*, 162 (May, 1896), 588–593; Henry D. Lloyd, "The Populists at St. Louis," *Review of Reviews*, 14 (September, 1896), 298–303, an account of the Populist convention which nominated Bryan and Watson; Fred E. Haynes, "The New Sectionalism," *Quarterly Journal of Economics*, 10 (April, 1896), 269–295, recognizes the debtor status of the West and South; C. F. Emerick, "An Analysis of Agricultural Discontent in the United States," *Political Science Quarterly*, 11 (September, December, 1896), 433–463, 601–639, 12 (March, 1897), 93–127.

Lively popular accounts of the period may be found in Harry Thurston Peck, *Twenty Years of the Republic* (New York, 1906), chapters 10 and 11, and Mark Sullivan, *The Turn of the Century* (New York, 1926). In fiction, Ignatius Donnelly, *Caesar's Column* (Chicago, 1890), drew a frightening picture of what might happen if the demands of the farmer-labor party were not heeded, and his *The Golden Bottle; or, the Story of Ephraim Benezet of Kansas* (New York, 1892) dealt with various reforms, including free silver. An insight into the feelings of prairie folk may be obtained from two other novels: William Allen White, *A Certain Rich Man* (New York, 1909), and Hamlin Garland, *A Son of the Middle Border* (New York, 1917).

II. THE FREE SILVER ISSUE. For a general understanding of the question, consult Davis R. Dewey, *Financial History of the United States* (8th edition, New York, 1922), and Alonzo B. Hepburn, *A History of Currency in the United States* (New York, 1915).

A selection from contemporary books and articles will give an idea of the running debate of the 1890's: Frank W. Taussig, *The Silver Situation in the United States* (New York, 1892), an intelligent survey; J. Laurence Laughlin, *The History of Bimetallism in the United States* (New York, 1892), strongly upholds the gold standard; Francis A. Walker, "The Free Coinage of Silver," *Journal of Political Economy*, 1 (March, 1893), 163–178, a warning against silver monometallism; William H. Harvey, *Coin's Financial School*, the most widely circulated pro-silver tract; E. Benjamin Andrews, *An Honest Dollar* (Hartford, 1894), by a convinced bimetallist; J. Laurence Laughlin, *Facts about Money* (Chicago, 1895), includes a debate with Harvey; Ignatius Donnelly, *The American People's Money* (Chicago, 1895), by a Populist leader; Arthur I. Fonda, *Honest Money* (New York, 1895), a conservative answer; Willard Fisher, " 'Coin' and His Critics," *Quarterly Journal of Economics*, 10 (January, 1896), 187–208, "a plague on both your houses."

III. BIOGRAPHY OF BRYAN. Of primary importance are Bryan's own books: *The First Battle — A Story of the Campaign of 1896* (Chicago, 1896), *Speeches of William Jennings Bryan* (2 vols., New York, 1913), and *Memoirs* (Philadelphia, 1925), begun by Bryan and completed by his wife. Allen Johnson's article in the *Dictionary of American Biography* is competent but not colorful. Of many biographies the best are John Cuthbert Long, *Bryan, the Great Commoner* (New York, 1928), and Paxton Hibben, *The Peerless Leader* (New York, 1929). A brief but lively vignette may be found in Walter B. Pitkin, *The Psychology of Happiness* (New York, 1929; reissued as *The Secret of Happiness*, 1933), 84–94.

IV. OTHER POLITICAL LEADERS. The following works deal with figures high in Democratic or Populist councils: Waldo Ralph Browne, *Altgeld of Illinois* (New

York, 1924); Harvey Wish, "John P. Altgeld and the Background of the Campaign of 1896," *Mississippi Valley Historical Review*, 24 (March, 1938), 503–518; see also Vachel Lindsay's poem "The Eagle That Is Forgotten"; John D. Hicks, "The Political Career of Ignatius Donnelly," *Mississippi Valley Historical Review*, 8 (June–September, 1921), 80–132; Elmer Ellis, *Henry Moore Teller, Defender of the West* (Caldwell, Idaho, 1941), Silver Republican; Francis Butler Simkins, *The Tillman Movement in South Carolina* (Durham, N. C., 1926); Fred E. Haynes, *James Baird Weaver* (Iowa City, 1919); William W. Brewton, *The Life of Thomas E. Watson* (Atlanta, Ga., 1926), or better, C. Vann Woodward, *Tom Watson: Agrarian Rebel* (New York, 1938).

For Republicans and Gold Democrats, see the following: Herbert Croly, *Marcus Alonzo Hanna* (New York, 1912), and Thomas Beer, *Hanna* (New York, 1929); Charles S. Olcott, *The Life of William McKinley* (2 vols., Boston, 1916); Robert M. McElroy, *Grover Cleveland* (2 vols., New York, 1923); and Allan Nevins, *Grover Cleveland* (New York, 1932).

V. THE AFTERMATH OF WESTERN RADICALISM. While the Populist party passed from the national scene, many of its progressive ideas were embodied in the developing concept of the welfare state. The materials which follow illuminate various aspects of this thesis: Frank Basil Tracy, "Rise and Doom of the Populist Party," *Forum*, 16 (October, 1893), 241–250, a vicious attack anticipating the collapse of the People's party; William A. Peffer, "The Passing of the People's Party," *North American Review*, 166 (January, 1898), 12–23, speculation as to what may still be saved; Charles M. Harger, "New Era in the Middle West," *Harpers' Magazine*, 97 (July, 1898), 276–282, describes the end of the land boom and gradual recovery; Marion Butler, "The People's Party," *Forum*, 28 (February, 1900), 658–662, by the chairman of the Populist National Committee; Thomas E. Watson, "The People's Party's Appeal," *Independent*, 57 (October 13, 1904), 829, and "Why I Am Still a Populist," *Review of Reviews*, 38 (September, 1908), 303–306, by the party's most eminent die-hard; Louis B. Schmidt, "Some Significant Aspects of the Agrarian Revolution in the United States," *Iowa Journal of History and Politics*, 28 (July, 1920), 371–395; Charles A. Beard, *American Government and Politics* (4th edition, New York, 1924), a notable statement concerning the perseverance of Populist doctrines; William Allen White, "The End of an Epoch," *Scribner's Magazine*, 79 (June, 1926), 561–570; James A. Woodburn, "Western Radicalism in American Politics," *Mississippi Valley Historical Review*, 13 (September, 1926), 143–168; and Joseph C. Manning, *The Fadeout of Populism* (New York, 1928).